SOURCE BOOK OF

AFRICAN AND AFRO-AMERICAN

MATERIALS FOR MUSIC EDUCATORS

James A. Standifer

Barbara Reeder

*CMP*₇

CONTEMPORARY MUSIC PROJECT

Cover: A photograph of the wooden portrait statue of King Bom Bosh, the 96th *nyimi* (ruler) of the Bakuba or Bushango, a tribe of the Congo.

From the beginning of the seventeenth century, it was the practice to carve a portrait of each king during his lifetime which, after his death, had a most important function in preserving the continuity of the royal power and wisdom in his successor.

Bom Bosh reigned about 1650-1660, and there is very little doubt that this is the actual statue made in his life-time.

Permission to reproduce photo of this statue granted through the courtesy of The Brooklyn Museum, gift of Mr. and Mrs. Robert E. Blum, Mr. and Mrs. Alastair Bradley Martin, Donald M. Oenslager, Mrs. Florence E. Blum Fund.

Photo credits: Cover, pages 1 and 45, Center for Ethnic Music, Howard University, Vada Butcher, director. Page 121, the Music Educators Journal of the Music Educators National Conference.

Copyright © 1972
Contemporary Music Project
Music Educators National Conference

All rights reserved

Library of Congress
Catalog Number: 72-77987

First printing, 1972
Printed in the U.S.A.

Let Others Dream
What They Dream
I Dream
Music

I Am A Source Person
My Body
Its Height With Length And Color
Is My House
The Earth
The Universe
My Place

Call Me What You Will
Call My Music
Music.
—ARTHUR CUNNINGHAM

CONTENTS

FOREWORD

The reader who is acquainted with the programs and publications of the Contemporary Music Project might be puzzled by CMP's involvement in the subject of this volume. And yet this subject is indeed appropriate to the concept of comprehensive musicianship which cultivates an understanding of a wide variety of musical styles. The refinement and promotion of this concept is the basis for the Project's activities.

The classroom experiences described in Parts I and II illustrate the potential of *the common elements approach* advocated by CMP as the most advantageous way to study music of diverse styles and cultures. The Project has encouraged and supported programs, through its teacher fellowship awards, that apply this approach to a wide and varied repertoire.

The common elements approach provides an effective "tool" for developing a sense of security in handling a wide variety of music according to individual backgrounds and abilities. The elements of sound—their organization and interaction—serve as the carrier of knowledge and understandings to new experiences. Thus, this approach affords both teacher and student a greater amount of musical confidence in developing the components of comprehensive musicianship.

This Source Book is the result of support given to each author to experiment with the concept of comprehensive musicianship in urban music education, Mrs. Reeder through African music in the secondary schools of Seattle and Dr. Standifer through Afro-American music in the secondary schools of Philadelphia. As a result of these experiences and their subsequent work as consultants, writers and resource leaders, Professors Reeder and Standifer found a great need for materials such as those reported in this volume. It is their hope, and that of CMP, that this information will be of help to the classroom teacher, the music specialist, and instructors of methods classes, in guiding them and their students toward an increased understanding of these musical styles which are so much a part of their environment.

The concept of comprehensive musicianship does not reject the importance of areas of specialization as they contribute to the goals of a more complete musicianship. This book can serve, therefore, as a much needed resource in strengthening the study of African and Afro-American music, an area of specialization that has been neglected in most traditional study programs.

The Contemporary Music Project is pleased to make this Source Book available, for it represents an outgrowth of two of its experimental programs and, we believe, a new impetus for exploring further the common elements approach as a means for more comprehensive experiences in music.

Norman Dello Joio, *Chairman*
Robert J. Werner, *Director*

INTRODUCTION

A new breed of music educator is emerging on the current educational scene, whose awareness of the importance of teaching and studying the musics of a kaleidoscope of world cultures is observable in many regions. Credit for this phenomenon cannot be awarded to the college music curriculum nor to the music education divisions of various school systems, though efforts are being made in these areas to improve the quality and to broaden the base of content in the music curriculum. Rather, we must recognize the impact of a more perceptive and demanding student population and citizenry.

These factors, among others, make it plain that traditional music curricula which is mainly concerned with the last two or three hundred years of European music is no longer adequate for today's schools. As David Willoughby so aptly stated, "Basic music studies must be considered a segment of world culture and can no longer be provincial, devoted only to classical music of the Western world, for this music represents a relatively small segment of time in a relatively small geographical section of the globe."

This new breed of music educator, because of this emerging awareness, will be cognizant of world musics and of the need for their inclusion in music curricula. Specifically, to view the role of black music in American society through value judgments appropriate to the cultural context, hopefully, will provide alternatives in musical expression for students.

When students tell us that the music we teach and the methods we use are irrelevant and ineffectual, music educators cannot simply sit back with eyes closed and ears turned backward. Clearly, each music teacher's responsibility is to increase his awareness of the aesthetic needs not only of all his students, but also of the entire community which he serves. His teaching must relate to these needs.

A critical issue facing music educators is the inner city. They are not properly prepared to cope with the severe problems created by poor housing, unemployment, poverty, and other intolerable conditions that exist in cities throughout the United States. The Tanglewood Symposium of 1967, sponsored by the Music Educators National Conference, declared that teachers must provide learning opportunities that meet individual needs and the needs of a society plagued by the consequences of changing values, generation gaps, racial and international tensions and the challenges of a new leisure.

In an attempt to meet these needs, the Music Division of the Seattle Public Schools and the Philadelphia Public Schools with the Music Department of Temple University prepared proposals to CMP for the formulation of new curricula and materials for revitalizing music learning in urban schools.

We are grateful to the Contemporary Music Project for sponsoring and providing the funds for these projects. Dr. Standifer and Mrs. Reeder were released part time from their duties to work with pupils and teachers in the public schools. A steering committee of teachers and interested black professional musicians was organized in each city. This new and exciting publication is a result of these programs.

The content of this book is another attempt of the Contemporary Music Project to present a broad scope of music to the teaching fraternity. It is within the philosophy and structure of CMP to bring this publication to the entire profession, and therefore it seems appropriate that they provide this material as part of their curricular approach.

The two authors—one white, one black—symbolize an important need today, which is to deal with these problems by working together toward common goals.

Louis G. Wersen
Director, Division of Music
Philadelphia Public Schools
President, MENC, 1966-1968

Jack E. Schaeffer
Supervisor of Music Education
Seattle Public Schools
President, MENC, 1972-1974

PREFACE

Music is a universal phenomenon. It is not a universal language. It communicates in ways that cannot always be adequately described. Analytical tools that were developed for the musical expression of one culture usually are inappropriate to clarify the sound events of another. Music of a culture should not be evaluated in terms other than those employed by its practitioners, for there is no "ideal" music culture.

In the music of all cultures it is possible to isolate elements common to all musical sounds, elements such as pitch, loudness, tone qualities unique to specific sound-producing devices, relative durations, density and texture. Through personal contact and involvement in music study which focuses on the organization and interaction of these elements, insights can be gained into the musical expressions of one's own culture as well as that of another. One's perception of any culture's musical expression seems to be in direct proportion to the extent of personal experience with the music of that culture. This direct contact with elements common to various music cultures can lead to the development of musically sensitive individuals and can act as a catalyst for growth towards openness in musical and pedagogical attitudes.

Music reflects the cultural consensus of a particular group of human beings. This consensus imposes a cultural filter through which music is heard and experienced. Sounds which do not give meaning to the listener become sources of his irritation and disorientation.

This unpalatable experience is a prime cause of musical isolation and, indeed, isolation of one culture from another, which admittedly may have significant creative and stylistic advantages. However, factors intrinsic to this phenomenon also create serious difficulties for developing understanding and respect among music cultures. This isolation has encouraged the independent development of imprisoning conventions which serve as barriers to positive attitudes, learnings and cultural insights. The concept of comprehensive musicianship seeks to break down these barriers.

There is evidence that we are ready to develop constructive attitudes toward divergences in musical traditions. These divergences, seen as opportunities for expanding our ideas of beauty, become resources for musical understanding and growth. In our profession we are beginning to understand that these divergences are responses to history and to a cultural matrix, not simply to an acceptance of the dictates of fashion. Already, as professionals and as human beings, we are less provincial regarding the fare of the music consumer. We are discovering that analytical tools which clarify the musical expression of one culture may not be useful when applied to the music of another. We have learned that priorities and functions of music in one culture may be different from those of another. A culture is given vitality and distinction through its unique methods of expression, which make the musical processes of one culture different from those of another, with each retaining validity. Our cultural filters are beginning to allow us to operate in ways that *motivate* rather than *inhibit* comprehensive growth and understanding.

It seems plausible that to avoid many complexities of musical traditions as well as gross errors in perception one should approach the study of music of other cultures in terms of sound. The elements of sound may provide us with the "hook upon which to hang our ear," as the nineteenth-century aesthetician, Eduard Hanslich, described it.

This is to say that African and Afro-American music should be studied comprehensively and not with the narrowed eye of Western art-music criticism nor with analytical tools that are compatible only with music of the Western European heritage. A sound-oriented, common elements approach will admit the possibility of similarities as well as the realization of differences among African, Afro-American and Euro-American musical traditions. To study the many culture areas in Africa and the broad continuum of Afro-American music, the organization and interaction of the elements of sound should be experienced in ways that are comprehensive and that provide the least cultural bias.

Two examples follow:

1. In the Western European art-music tradition, exact pitch is very important. Students will apologize instantly for playing a wrong pitch, although mistakes in duration, timbre or loudness may be apparent in their performance. In some music cultures, accurate pitch is equally important but the pitches are not those of the Euro-American tradition. Pitch organization may seem very inaccurate or at least ambiguous to musicians trained in the tradition of Western art music, but to become "exact" according to the latter tradition might be inappropriate to performance in the context of another culture. If pitch organization in music of other cultures seems repetitive or unclear to "Western ears," it is because a more restricted cultural filter is operating.

2. Vocal quality is one of many examples of timbral differences among cultures. The transfer of one culture's ideal vocal quality to the performance in the context of another might be inappropriate. This, of course, applies to rock, rhythm and blues, liturgical church music and opera as well as to vocal music of cultures outside of the Western art-music influence. In one area of Africa, it is considered vital that a person's voice reflects his personality. A group of singers sounds clearly like

a group of individuals. To attempt to create a vocal blend would deny this individuality and thus be inappropriate in the context of this culture.

The materials in this Source Book should be viewed with factors such as these in mind. This publication is intended to provide encouragement to teachers to include music of other traditions, particularly African and Afro-American, in music curricula. Music educators who are not trained in these traditions will gain deeper insights through increased exposure to this music.

Because of the special nature of many of the listings in this Source Book, the following clarifications must be made:

1. Some of the materials reflect attitudes of an earlier era and must be used with that in mind.

2. Sources which contain transcriptions should be used cautiously. In much black music, notation, if used at all, serves only to remind musicians of particular tonal and rhythmic configurations. This music is derived from an aural tradition and is to be re-created, not reproduced as in the Western art-music tradition.

3. Because of the vastness and complexity of the subject, the content is not exhaustive. The following criteria of selection were applied:
   a. Authenticity and accuracy
   b. Breadth reflective of the cultures involved
   c. Successful use in music classes
   d. Maximum information from one source
   e. Availability
   f. Background material

4. Many recordings were excluded from the Discography because of inferior qualities of reproduction, although especially important recordings were included in spite of technical imperfections. Purchasing recordings from companies found most often in the Discography will help music educators avoid selecting recordings which are not authentic examples of the culture they represent.

5. This Source Book is intended to be used as follows:
   a. Reference source for students and teachers
   b. Motivation for teachers who have not included black musical contributions in curricula
   c. Acquisition suggestions for librarians
   d. Sources for continued professional growth for teachers

6. This work contains both annotated and non-annotated entries. The annotated sources are those with which the authors are more familiar, having used them in music classes more frequently than

other entries. Non-annotated entries are included to demonstrate the scope of materials available.

7. The classroom experiences included in Parts I and II are intended to support the source materials by offering suggested procedures for incorporating many of them in music classes. These descriptions depict ideas on which the teacher's understandings of many musical traditions and of certain classroom strategies can be based.

James A. Standifer
Barbara Reeder

March 1972

ACKNOWLEDGMENTS

In the preparation of any book such as this and particularly in one where it is necessary to research sources that are not readily available, the authors realize the debt they owe to the many people who have provided assistance in the effort to make this source book of as great a value to the reader as possible. Among those persons who have offered suggestions regarding the original projects upon which this book was based and the subsequent preparation of the manuscript resulting from them are: Robert Garfias, Robert Kauffman, Joe Brazil, Billy Jackson, Lynne Jessup, Max Brandt and Edward Lee; also Mary Asher, MaryAnn Tyler, Natalie Hinderas, Don Rothermel and members of the Committee on Urban Studies in Music Education in Philadelphia.

With the accumulation of this material it became imperative that the manuscript be reviewed by a number of knowledgeable people. We are most appreciative to the following colleagues for their professional expertise: Verna Avery, William Grant Still, David N. Baker, Jr., La Deva Davis, James Lewis, Ewa Eko, Gorman Duffet and Jacquelyn Boswell; also Vada Butcher, Alan Merriam, Klaus Wachsmann, Hall Overton, James Dapogny, Clark Terry and Russell Sanjek. If we have not fully satisfied all of the requirements of this undertaking, it is the responsibility of the authors and not of those who so graciously gave of their time to refine our efforts.

The preparation of this manuscript with all of its many requirements was a complex problem indeed, and the authors are greatly indebted to David Willoughby, of the CMP staff, for both his editorial assistance and the supervision that he gave throughout the book's preparation.

Special recognition is given to music educators in the United States who have had to create their own bibliographies and related resources without assistance or encouragement and who may know of many items that should be included in later revisions of this information.

James A. Standifer
Barbara Reeder

PART I

African Music

PART I

BIBLIOGRAPHY

Books on Africa

The books in this section include general historical, anthropological and cultural information on Africa.

Achebe, Chinua. *Things Fall Apart.* New York: Astor-Honor, 1959.
   A novel concerning the effect of the arrival of a white missionary in an Ibo community in the Nigerian hinterland.

Anene, Joseph C. and Godfrey N. Brown (eds.). *Africa in the Nineteenth and Twentieth Centuries: A Handbook for Teachers and Students.* London: Thomas Nelson & Sons, Ltd., 1966 (Reprinted 1968).
   Has been used as a text in history courses at Ibadan University, Ibadan, Nigeria.

Beier, Ulli (ed.). *African Poetry.* Cambridge: Cambridge University Press, 1966.
   A short anthology that contains poems from different parts of Africa. Explanatory notes included.

Bohannan, Paul. *Africa and Africans.* Garden City, New York: Doubleday & Co., Inc., 1964.
   A paperback book putting African culture in perspective for western readers by examining facts about Africa and the Western myths that have obscured them.

Davidson, Basil. *Africa in History.* New York: Macmillan, 1969. Revised edition (from 1966).
   With erudition and insight, Davidson underscores Africa's ability to take care of itself long before European rule. This is a useful history of the African continent.

Herskovits, Melville and W. R. Bascom (eds.). *Continuity and Change in African Cultures.* Chicago: University of Chicago Press, 1959.
   A group of essays discussing aspects of African culture, as viewed by authorities in linguistics, art, music, history and anthropology.

Hunter, Bruce. *Tribal Map of Negro Africa.* New York: Man and Nature Publications, 1956.
   Lists African tribal groups in alphabetical order and keys them to the accompanying map.

Jahn, Janheinz. *Muntu: A New Approach to African Culture*. New York: Grove Press, Inc., 1961.

> Provides a philosophical framework for African studies. It is somewhat difficult to read but furnishes an essential cultural vantage point.

Jahn, Janheinz. *Through African Doors: Experiences and Encounters in West Africa*. New York: Grove Press, Inc., 1969.

> A sensitive description of people, sights and sounds, which provides a cultural perspective and is easy to read.

Larson, C. R. (ed.). *African Short Stories: A Collection of Contemporary African Writing*. New York: Collier-Macmillan Library Service, 1970.

Murdock, George Peter. *Africa: Its People and Their Cultural History*. New York: McGraw-Hill Book Co., 1959.

> An ethnological source book that presents a cultural-historical base line for a study of the people of Africa. It deals with food-producing activities, housing and settlement patterns, kinship and marriage, forms of social and political organizations, and population figures for hundreds of culture areas in Africa. An accompanying map shows the approximate territorial boundaries of the various tribes and nations described in the text.

Oliver, Roland and Anthony Atmore. *Africa Since 1800*. London: Cambridge University Press, 1967.

> A readable history of Africa in paperback that includes helpful maps.

Oliver, Roland and J. D. Fage. *A Short History of Africa*. Baltimore: Penguin, 1962 (Reprinted 1968).

> A concise statement of the history of the continent. Very good for providing historical perspective.

Senghor, Leopold Sedar. *Selected Poems*. New York: Atheneum, 1969.

> A collection of poems by the President of Senegal from the years 1945 to 1962.

Turnbull, Colin. *Forest People*. New York: Simon and Schuster, Inc., 1961.

> A description of the life of the pygmies in the Ituri Forest, which is interesting to read and very warm in spirit.

Webster, J. B. and A. A. Boahen with H. O. Idowu. *History of West Africa: The Revolutionary Years: 1815 to Independence*. New York: Praeger Publishers, 1967.

> An excellent source containing readable information on the history of West Africa.

Books on Music

Blacking, John. *Venda Children's Songs.* Johannesburg: Witwatersrand University Press, 1967.

Carrington, J. F. *Talking Drums of Africa.* Westport, Connecticut: Negro Universities Press, 1969 (Reprint).
A very detailed explanation of the function, techniques and processes used by one culture area for communicating by means of "talking" drums.

Gwangwa, Jonas and E. John Miller, Jr. *The World of African Song: Miriam Makeba.* Chicago: Quadrangle Books, 1971.
Introduces the reader to the experience of African song in the unique style of Miriam Makeba. Each song appears with information about the song and suggestions for appropriate instrumental accompaniment.

Jones, A. M. *African Music in Northern Rhodesia and Some Other Places.* Livingstone, Rhodesia: Rhodes-Livingstone Museum, 1949.

Jones, A. M. *Studies in African Music.* 2 Volumes. London: Oxford University Press, 1959.
Volume One discusses the musical examples transcribed in Volume Two. The scores which appear in Volume Two indicate as closely as possible, using Western notation, the relationship of sound events in West African music.

Jones, A. M. and L. Kombe. *The Icila Dance, Old Style; A Study in African Music and Dance of the Lala Tribe of Northern Rhodesia.* Roodeport: Longmans, Green, 1952.
Drum making is discussed along with descriptions and illustrations of performance practices with drums, dancing and singing.

King, Anthony. *Yoruba Sacred Music from Ekiti.* Ibadan, Nigeria: Ibadan University Press, 1961.

Kirby, Percival R. *The Musical Instruments of the Native Races of South Africa.* Johannesburg: Witwatersrand University Press, 1968.

Merriam, Alan P. *The Anthropology of Music.* Evanston: Northwestern University Press, 1964.
Discusses problems and procedures in the study of ethnic music. Highly recommended.

Nettl, Bruno. *Folk and Traditional Music of the Western Continents.* Englewood Cliffs, New Jersey: Prentice-Hall, 1965.

Nketia, J. H. Kwabena. *African Music in Ghana.* Evanston: Northwestern University Press, 1963.

Written as a general introduction to the music of Ghana, this book outlines types of folk music, kinds of ensembles and the content of the music; it includes musical examples which illustrate the stylistic features of the music discussed.

Nketia, J. H. Kwabena. *Drumming in Akan Communities of Ghana.* New York: Thomas Nelson & Sons, 1963.

A study of drumming, its musical and social aspects, structure and organization. It also contains a section on the construction of drums and several notated examples of drumming patterns.

Nketia, J. H. Kwabena. *Folk Songs of Ghana.* Legon: University of Ghana Press, 1963.

Contains traditional songs from Ghana which are transcribed and grouped by musical type. Includes background information.

Tracey, Hugh. *Chopi Musicians, Their Music, Poetry and Instruments.* London: Oxford University Press, 1948.

Articles on Music

Aning, B. S. "Factors That Shape and Maintain Folk Music in Ghana," *International Folk Music Journal,* Vol. 20 (1968), pp. 13-17.

Blacking, John. "Tonal Organization in the Music of Two Venda Initiation Schools," *Ethnomusicology,* Vol. 14 (January 1970).

Composer (Journal of the Composers Guild of Great Britain, 4 St. James Square, London, SW1, England), No. 19 (Spring 1966).

A series of papers on African music presented by such scholars as J. H. Kwabena Nketia, Hugh Tracey and Fela Sowande at the Commonwealth Music Conference, Liverpool, September 1965.

England, Nicholas M. "Bushman Counterpoint," *International Folk Music Journal,* Vol. 19 (1967), pp. 58-65.

Euba, Akin. "In Search of a Common Musical Language in Africa," *Interlink, the Nigerian Quarterly.* Howard University, Project in African Music, 1969, pp. 85-89 (other pertinent articles in same source).

Euba, Akin. "Multiple Pitch Lines in Yoruba Choral Music," *International Folk Music Journal,* Vol. 19 (1967), pp. 66-71.

Jones, A. M. "African Rhythm," *Africa* (Journal of the International African Institute), Vol. 24 (1954), pp. 26-47. London: Oxford University Press.

Jones, A. M. "East and West, North and South," *African Music,* Vol. 1, No. 1 (1954), pp. 57-62.

Kauffman, Robert. "Some Aspects of Aesthetics in the Shona Music of Rhodesia," *Ethnomusicology,* Vol. 13 (September 1969), pp. 507-511.

King, Anthony. "Employment of the 'Standard Pattern' in Yoruba Music," *African Music,* Vol. 2, No. 3 (1960), pp. 51-54.

Kubik, Gerhard. "The Alo-Yoruba Story Songs," *African Music,* Vol. 4, No. 2 (1958), pp. 10-32.

Lunsonga, Cajetan. "Bemba Music," *African Music,* Vol. 3, No. 4 (1965), pp. 26-28.

Merriam, Alan P. "African Music Re-examined in the Light of New Materials from the Belgian Congo and Ruanda-Urundi," *Zaire,* Vol. 7 (1953), pp. 245-253.

Merriam, Alan P. "African Music," in *Continuity and Change in African Cultures,* William R. Bascom and Melville J. Herskovitz. Chicago: University of Chicago Press, 1959.

Merriam, Alan P. "Characteristics of African Music," *International Folk Music Journal,* Vol. 11 (1959), pp. 13-19.

Nikiprowetzky, Tolia. "The Griots of Senegal and Their Instruments," *International Folk Music Journal,* Vol. 15 (1963), pp. 79-82.

Nketia, J. H. Kwabena. "Changing Traditions of Folk Music in Ghana," *International Folk Music Journal,* Vol. 11 (1959), pp. 31-36.

Nketia, J. H. Kwabena. "Modern Trends in Ghana Music," *African Music,* Vol. 1, No. 4 (1957), pp. 13-17.

Nketia, J. H. Kwabena. "The Hocket Technique in African Music," *International Folk Music Journal,* Vol. 14 (1962), pp. 44-52.

Nketia, J. H. Kwabena. "The Music of Africa," *Journal of Human Relations.* Central State College, Wilberforce, Ohio, Vol. 8, No. 3 and 4 (1960), pp. 730-738.

Nketia, J. H. Kwabena. "The Role of the Drummer in Akan Society," *African Music,* Vol. 1, No. 1 (1954), pp. 34-43.

Nketia, J. H. Kwabena. "The Problem of Meaning in African Music," *Ethnomusicology,* Vol. 6 (January 1962), pp. 1-7.

Nketia, J. H. Kwabena. "Traditional and Contemporary Idioms of African Music," *International Folk Music Journal,* Vol. 16 (1964), pp. 34-37.

Rycroft, David. "Nguni Vocal Polyphony," *International Folk Music Journal,* Vol. 19 (1967), pp. 88-103.

Schneider, Marius. "Tone and Tune in West African Music," *Ethnomusicology,* Vol. 5 (September 1961), pp. 204-215.

Smith, Edna M. "Musical Training in Tribal West Africa," *African Music,* Vol. 3, No. 1 (1962), pp. 6-10.

Sowande, Fela. Six papers on aspects of Nigerian music. New York: Broadcasting Foundation of America, 1962-1967.

Books on Musical Instruments

Boone, Olga. *Les Tambours du Congo Belge et du Ruanda-Urundi.* Annales du Musíc du Congo belge, Tervuren (Belgique), 1951.
Written in French but includes many photographs.

Dietz, Betty W. and M. B. Olatunji. *Musical Instruments of Africa.* New York: John Day, 1965.
A useful and attractively illustrated book that deals with the four main classifications of West African instruments. An accompanying record gives examples of the instruments.

Echezona, William W. C. "Musical Instruments in Ibo Culture." Unpublished Ph.D. dissertation, Michigan State University, 1963. See Echezona's article on this topic in *Music Educator's Journal,* Vol. 50 (April-May 1964), p. 23.

Kirby, Percival R. *The Musical Instruments of the Native Races of South Africa.* Johannesburg: Witwatersrand University Press, 1968.
The descriptive text providing detailed information about the categories of instruments in this area is followed by photographs of the instruments.

Laurentry, J. S. *Les Cordophones du Congo Belge et du Ruanda-Urundi.* Annales du Musíc du Congo belge, Tervuren (Belgique), 1960.
This book, written in French, contains photographs of instruments.

Marcuse, Sibyl. *Musical Instruments: A Comprehensive Dictionary.* New York: Doubleday, 1964.
A very complete listing of musical instruments from all over the world. Entries are accompanied by descriptions. Highly recommended.

Nketia, J. H. Kwabena. *Our Drums and Drummers*. Accra: Ghana Publishing House, 1968.

Written in English for African school children, this small book is a readable discussion of drums in Ghanian culture.

Thieme, Darius L. "A Descriptive Catalogue of Yoruba Musical Instruments." Unpublished Ph.D. dissertation, Catholic University of America, 1969.

Trowell, Margaret and K. P. Wachsmann. *Tribal Crafts of Uganda*. New York: Oxford University Press, 1953.

Includes many photographs and simple line drawings of the musical instruments of Uganda with other pertinent information.

Books on Dance

Ballif, Noël. *Dancers of God*. Translated from the French by James Cameron. London: Sidwick & Jackson, 1955.

Brelsford, W. V. *African Dances of Northern Rhodesia*. Livingstone: Rhodes-Livingstone Museum, 1948.

Darbois, Dominique. *African Dance*. London: Hamlin Publishing Group, 1963.

Griaule, Marcel. *Masques Dogons*. Paris: Institut d'ethnologie, 1938.

Hambly, Wilfrid Dyson. *Tribal Dancing and Social Development*. London: H. F. & G. Witherby, 1926.

Jones, A. M. and L. Kombe. *The Icila Dance, Old Style: A Study in African Music and Dance of the Lala Tribe of Northern Rhodesia*. Roodepoort: Longmans, Green, 1952.

Richards, Audrey I. *Chisungu: A Girl's Initiation Ceremony Among the Bemba of Northern Rhodesia*. New York: Grove Press, 1956.

Sachs, Curt. *World History of Dance*. New York: W. W. Norton, 1963.

Tracey, Hugh. *African Dances of the Witwatersrand Gold Mines*. Johannesburg: African Music Society (distributed by Constantia Booksellers and Publishers), 1952.

Tremearne, Arthur J. N. *The Ban of the Bori*. London: Heath, Cranton & Ousley, Ltd., 1914.

Tucker, Archibald Norman. *Tribal Music and Dancing in Southern Sudan*. London: W. Reeves, Ltd., 1933.

Articles on Dance

Blacking, John. "Musical Expeditions of the Venda," *African Music Society*. Vol. 3, No. 1 (1962), pp. 54-78, illustrated.

Chilkovsky, Nadia. "Techniques for the Choreologist," *Ethnomusicology*. Vol. 5, No. 2 (1961), pp. 121-127.

Evans-Pritchard, E. E. "The Dance," *Africa*. Vol. 1 (1928), pp. 446-462.

Hanna, Judith Lynne. "Africa's New Traditional Dance," *Ethnomusicology*. Vol. 9 (January 1965), pp. 13-21.

Harper, Peggy. "Dance in Nigeria," *Ethnomusicology*. Vol. 13 (May 1969), pp. 280-295.

Kurath, Gertrude P. "A Basic Vocabulary for Ethnic Dance Description," *American Anthropologist*. Vol. 56 (1954), pp. 1102-1103.

Kurath, Gertrude P. "Panorama of Dance Ethnology," *Current Anthropology*. Vol. 1 (1960), pp. 233-254, bibliography.

Mitchell, J. Clyde. "The Kelela Dance." Livingstone: Rhodes-Livingstone Papers, No. 27 (1956).

Nketia, J. H. Kwabena. "Possession Dances in African Societies," *International Folk Music Journal*. Vol. 9 (1957), pp. 4-9.

Nzekwu, Eunora. "Ibo Dancing," *Nigerian Magazine*, No. 73 (June 1962), pp. 35-42, illustrated.

Primus, Pearl. "African Dance," *African Heritage*. London: Collier-Macmillan, Ltd., 1964.

Segy, Ladislas. "The Mask in African Dance," *Negro History Bulletin*, Vol. 5 (February 1953), reprint.

Thompson, Robert Farris. "An Aesthetic of the Cool: West African Dance." *African Forum*. Vol. 2 (Fall 1966), pp. 85-102.

Waterman, Richard A. "Role of Dance in Human Society," in *Focus on Dance II: An Inter-disciplinary Search for Meaning in Movement*, Bettie Jane Wooten (ed.). Washington: American Association for Health, Physical Education and Recreation, 1962, pp. 47-50.

Wilson, Monica. "Nyakyusa Ritual and Symbolism," *American Anthropologist*. Vol. 56 (1954), pp. 228-247.

Books on Art

Allison, Philip. *African Stone Sculpture*. New York: Praeger, 1968.

Beier, Ulli. *African Mud Sculpture*. Cambridge, England: University Press, 1963.

Beier, Ulli. *Contemporary Art in Africa*. New York: Praeger, 1968.

Bravmann, René A. *West African Sculpture*. Seattle: University of Washington Press, 1970.

Duerden, Dennis. *African Art*. Feltham, Middlesex: Paul Hamlyn, 1968.

Eicher, Joanne Buholz. *African Dress: A Select and Annotated Bibliography of Sub-Saharan Countries*. East Lansing: Michigan State University, 1970.

Fagg, William Buller. *African Sculpture*. New York: Dutton, 1964.

Fagg, William Buller (ed.). *The Art of Central Africa: Sculpture and Tribal Masks*. New York: New American Library, 1967.

Fagg, William Buller and Eliot Elisofon. *The Sculpture of Africa: 405 Photographs*. Texts by William Fagg. Preface by Ralph Linton. Design by Bernard Quint. London: Thames & Hudson, 1958.

Gerbrands, Adrianus Alexander. *Art as an Element of Culture, Especially in Negro Africa*. Leiden: E. J. Brill, 1957.

Griaule, Marcel. *Masques Dogons*. Paris: Institut d'ethnologie, 1938.

Herskovits, Melville Jean. *The Background of African Art*. Denver, Colorado: Art Museum, 1945.

Leuzinger, Elsy. *The Art of Africa*. New York: Crown Publishers, 1960.

Radin, Paul. *African Folktales and Sculpture*. New York: Pantheon Books, 1964.

Sieber, Roy. *Sculpture of Black Africa*. Los Angeles: Los Angeles County Museum of Arts, 1968.

Trowell, Margaret. *African Design*. New York: Praeger, 1970.

Trowell, Margaret. *African and Oceanic Art*. New York: H. N. Abrams, 1968.

Wassing, René S. *African Art*. New York: H. N. Abrams, 1968.

Willett, Frank. *African Art: An Introduction*. New York: Praeger, 1971.

Books for Elementary Grades

The following entries might be helpful as supportive material for the study of African music. This abridged list merely indicates the increasing availability of books on Africa written for younger students.

Non-fiction

Dobler, Lavinia and W. A. Brown. *Great Rulers of the African Past.* Garden City, New York: Doubleday & Co., Inc., 1965.

Glubok, Shirley. *Art of Africa.* New York: Harper & Row Publishers, Inc., 1965.

Hughes, A. J. *East Africa: Kenya, Uganda, Tanzania.* Baltimore: Penguin Books, Inc., 1968.

Kaula, Edna Mason. *Bantu Africans.* New York: Franklin Watts, Inc., 1968.

Lacy, Leslie. *Black Africa on the Move.* New York: Franklin Watts, Inc., 1969.

Fiction and Folklore

Aardema, Verna. *Tales from the Story Hat.* New York: Coward-McCann, Inc., 1960.
    Eight African folk tales.

Aardema, Verna. *More Tales from the Story Hat.* New York: Coward-McCann, Inc., 1966.
    Eleven African folk tales.

Barnes, Gregory. *Wind of Change.* New York: Lothrop, Lee & Shephard Co., 1968.

Courlander, Harold and G. Herzog. *Cow-Tail Switch.* New York: Holt, Rinehart & Winston, Inc., 1947.
    Seventeen humorous West African tales.

Courlander, Harold and A. K. Prempeh. *Hat-Shaking Dance and Other Tales from Ghana.* New York: Harcourt Brace Jovanovich, Inc., 1957.
    Twenty-one short folk tales of the Ashanti people of Ghana.

Courlander, Harold. *The King's Drum: and Other African Stories.* New York: Harcourt Brace Jovanovich, Inc., 1962.
    Collection of folk tales from different people and regions of Africa.

Haley, Gail E. *A Story, a Story.* New York: Atheneum Publishers, 1970.

Hamilton, Virginia. *Time-Ago Tales of Jahdu.* New York: Macmillan Company, 1969.

Kaula, Edna Mason. *African Village Folktales.* New York: World Publishing Company, 1968.

ADDITIONAL MATERIALS
Periodicals Regularly Containing Articles on African Music

Africa. Journal of the International African Institute. London: Oxford University Press.

African Affairs. Editorial Board, Royal African Society, 18 Northumberland Avenue, London, W.C. 2, England.

African Arts. Paul O. Proehl (ed.). Los Angeles: African Studies Center, University of California.

African Music. Journal of the African Music Society, P.O. Box 138, Roodeport, Transvaal, South Africa.

African Studies Bulletin. 409 W. 117th Street, New York, N.Y. 10027, 1958.

American Anthropologist. American Anthropological Association, 1530 P Street, N.W., Washington, D.C., 1899.

Current Anthropology. Sol Tax (ed.). 1126 East 59th Street, Chicago, Illinois, 1960.

Ethnomusicology. Journal of the Society for Ethnomusicology. Wesleyan University Press, Middletown, Connecticut.

International Folk Music Council Bulletin (or) *Journal.* Department of Music, Queens University, Kingston, Ontario.

Journal of American Folklore. William Hugh Jansen (ed.). American Folklore Society, University of Texas Press, Box 7819, Austin, Texas 78712.

Yearbook of the International Folk Music Council. Alexander L. Ringer (ed.). Urbana, Illinois: University of Illinois Press.

Tapes, Films and Film Strips
(see page 15 for addresses of film sources)

African Art and Culture. Prepared by Lucie B. McCandless. Pleasantville, New York: Schloat Productions, Inc. (A Prentice-Hall Company), 1968.
    Discs, filmstrips, teacher's guide. Illustrates musical instruments, art, textiles, jewelry and architecture of Africa.

Atumpan. Institute of Ethnomusicology, University of California at Los Angeles. 43 min./color.

A description of the construction and use of the "talking" master drum of the Ashanti. Filmed in Africa with narration by Mantle Hood.

Discovering the Music of Africa. Film Associates of California, 11559 Santa Monica Boulevard, Los Angeles, California 90025. 28 min./color.

A studio presentation which introduces instruments, signalling, poetry, dancing and ensemble playing related to West African music.

Duro Ladipo. NET. 16mm/30 min./black & white/sale $125/rental $5.40.

An introduction to Duro Ladipo, founder, director and composer of the Duro Ladipo Traveling Theatre Company of Oshogbo, Nigeria, and to his folk operas. The members of his company are seen performing in Yoruba villages.

Emerging Africa in the Light of Its Past. Prepared by Peter Hammond, Alan Merriam and Roy Sieber. Cultural History Research, Inc. New York: 3M International Microfilm Press, 1969.

Text, color filmstrip, tape and teacher guide for each unit:
"Land, People, and History"
"From Exploration to Independence"
"West Africa: Patterns of Traditional Culture"
"West Africa Today: Historical Perspectives"

The Hunters. Produced by the Film Study Center, Harvard University. Distributors: Contemporary Films. 76 min./color, 1959.

A documentary on the Bushmen of the Kalahari Desert.

Nigerian Art and Artists. New York: Broadcasting Foundation of America.
Tapes: 1. Three Programs
2. Compositions by Akin Euba
3. Music in Nigeria (lecture-demonstration by Fela Sowande)
4. Compositions by Akin Euba
5. Selected Compositions

Traditional African Instruments. Prepared by Willard Rhodes and Vada E. Butcher. Howard University, Project in African Music.
Slides, synchronized tape and script.

The Yoruba Talking Drum. Prepared by Fela Sowande. New York: Broadcasting Foundation of America.

A program for elementary and high schools illustrated with slides and tape recordings.

14

Film Sources

(for African and/or Afro-American films)

Africa Films
1860 Broadway
New York, N.Y. 10023

Bailey-Film Associates
11559 Santa Monica Boulevard
Los Angeles, Cal. 90025

Bell Telephone System
(contact local office) or
American Telephone & Telegraph
  Co.
Motion Picture Section
195 Broadway
New York, N.Y. 10007

Brandon Films, Inc.
200 West 57th Street
New York, N.Y. 10019

Children's Music Center
2858 Pico Boulevard
Los Angeles, Cal. 90023

Colonial Williamsburg
Film Distribution Section
Box 516
Williamsburg, Va. 23185

Contemporary Films, Inc.
267 West 25th Street
New York, N.Y. 10001

Dance Films, Inc.
130 West 57th Street
New York, N.Y. 10019

Film Associates of California
11559 Santa Monica Boulevard
Los Angeles, Cal. 90025

Institute of Ethnomusicology
University of California at Los
  Angeles
Los Angeles, Cal. 90024

International Film Bureau, Inc.
332 South Michigan Avenue
Chicago, Ill. 60604

McGraw-Hill Films
330 West 42nd Street
New York, N.Y. 10036

Michigan State University
WMSB Film Department
Michigan State University
East Lansing, Mich. 48823

Museum of Modern Art
11 West 53rd Street
New York, N.Y. 10019

NET Film Series
Audio Visual Center
Indiana University
Bloomington, Ind. 47401

Teaching Film Custodians, Inc.
25 West 43rd Street
New York, N.Y. 10036

Young American Films, Inc.
330 West 42nd Street
New York, N.Y. 10036

DISCOGRAPHY

The recordings of African music included in this section have been used in the authors' classrooms. Since new recordings are being issued, music educators should use this material for reference, rather than as a complete source of recordings of African music.

The following list represents sources of recordings of African music:
Anthology Record and Tape Corporation
135 West 41st Street
New York, N.Y. 10036

Disques OCORA
Office de cooperation radiophonique
46 Rue d'Amsterdam
Paris 8, France

Folkways Scholastic Records
50 West 44th Street
New York, N.Y. 10036

Merriam, Alan P. *African Music on LP: An Annotated Discography.* Evanston, Illinois: Northwestern University Press, 1970.

Nonesuch Records
15 Columbus Circle
New York, N.Y. 10023

"The Sound of Africa" Series of Long Playing Records.
Contains over two hundred listings of recordings of south, central and east African music, produced from 1948 to 1963 by the Recording Unit of the African Music Society, Hugh Tracey, Director. Collected and classified with card index by the International Library of African Music, P.O. Box 138, Roodepoort, Transvaal, South Africa.

UNESCO Anthology
International Record Industries, Inc.
32 Oxford Street
Lynn, Massachusetts 01901

Available Recordings

Africa East and West. Institute of Ethnomusicology, University of California at Los Angeles. ie records—ie 6751
This useful recording accompanies audio-visual material.
Side 1, "Music in Ghana," is not separated into bands so it is diffi-

cult to find selections. However, this recording is worth the effort involved.

In the second selection of "Music in Ghana," a traditional Ashanti poem is spoken by the drummer, played, then translated into English. Timbral layers can be clearly distinguished in the fourth selection which features an Ashanti Fontonfrom ensemble. The fifth selection includes solo passages performed singly, then in combination. In the sixth selection Ashanti "talking" trumpets illustrate communication by means of a tonal language.

"Music in Ghana" includes a Ga drum ensemble which illustrates both the buzzing "sound ideal" and application of the rhythmic function of two against three.

Side 2 includes selections of music from other parts of Africa.

Africa South of the Sahara. Folkways—FE 503. Introduction and Notes by Alan P. Merriam.

The Zulu Song from South Africa features regular clapping, as does the Swazi Song.

The Royal Drums of the Tutsi of Rwanda are a symbol of kingship. Drum batteries, other than those belonging to the Queen Mother, are not allowed. They are played only on special occasions. Six drums are played in this example of Tutsi Drums.

In the Hororo flute example the pattern implied by the melody is realized by the feet. Students could stay with these sounds by tapping their thighs.

In the Bambuti Songs the pygmies use falsetto yodeling, and the chorus enters with a four-note response with one repeated tone.

The Yoruba Song from Nigeria illustrates sporadic use of percussion to accent a unison song.

The Acoli Song from Uganda has an ostinato with subtle variations; in the Babinga Song from Central African Republic, students could accompany the low, regular, muffled sound with a steady clapping or stamping.

From Senegal, the Wolof drums illustrate layers of sound, interlocking drum patterns, and variable pitched drums. The *halam* example of the Wolof people from the Gambia-Senegal area illustrates a short, repeated and varied melodic pattern. The *halam* is a five-stringed instrument which is sometimes thought to be the progenitor of the banjo.

The African Mbira: Music of the Shona People of Rhodesia. Nonesuch Explorer Series—H 72043

Contains six examples of Shona music. The *mbira*, a metal-keyed instrument played with the thumbs and index finger of the right hand, is accompanied by the *hosho,* or rattle, and singing. Record notes provide information about the music, the instruments and the performance.

African Concert. Philips—PCC 214

With the exception of the "talking drum" example, a drum message from the Congo (side 1, band 5), this recording shows a strong Western influence and cannot be considered a source for examples authentic to the musical traditions of the Congo.

African Music. Laura C. Boulton. Folkways—FW 8852

The sound in this recording is not too good because of technical problems. However, the "Battle Signals on the Kru Peoples' War Horn" is special. In this example, messages are stated in Kru language, in English, then by the horn. Everyone gets very excited as they describe the battle action. Also, each of five secret society drums of the Bini people of Ondo Province in Nigeria are recorded separately, then together. This is one of too few recorded examples where the parts may be heard separately so we can better understand how they are combined, and how complex the combinations are.

African Story Songs. University of Washington Press.

Abraham Dumisani Maraire tells stories and sings *ngano* (story songs) belonging to the musical tradition of the Shona people of Rhodesia. Includes the Shona words and English translation of the *ngano.*

Anthologie de la Musique du Tchad. OCORA-OCR 36-37-38

OCR 36 Les Sara: In the Kaba music recorded at Bekan, there are eight men, each blowing a bamboo whistle. Each whistle produces a fixed note and as each enters in succession a melody is formed. The xylophone enters, keeping to the melodic design, while whistles continue to play. The whole ensemble is joined by two drums and occasionally by the horn.

OCR 37 Le Mayo—kebbi occidental: The Massa music recorded at Koumi is a song accompanied by three four-stringed bow harps. The singer himself plays one of the harps. The rhythmic base is provided by the harpist's repeated striking of his forearm against the sound-box of the instrument.

OCR 38 Population Islamisées: In the Kanembou music recorded at Fort-Lamy, the *ghaita* player makes his instrument "talk." Those knowing the language and how to transpose it can easily understand what the *ghaita* is saying.

Ba-Benzele Pygmies. An Anthology of African Music (UNESCO Collection). Bärenreiter Musicaphone—BM 30 L 2303

Features Pygmy music from the Congo. It contains an example of a man playing a flute with a single pitch. Between the notes played on the flute, he sings a tune. This alternation between voice and flute illustrates the principle of interlocking sounds which is found in other parts of Africa.

Bantu Music from British East Africa. Vol. X—Columbia World Library of Folk and Primitive Music. KL-213

In the Ntimbo Drum Rhythms of the Bunyoro in Uganda, official drummers play little goblet-shaped drums with membranes of the finest water-lizard skins.

Entenga drummers of the Ganda people of Uganda play Nsiriba Ya Munange Katego, a drum tune performed on a set of fifteen *entenga* (tuned conical drums). Four men perform upon a set of twelve drums, tuned to two octaves of a pentatonic scale while two men accompany them on the three bass drums.

One of the fifteen movements of the Ngodo dance of the Chopi people of Mozambique is also on this record. The xylophones are made in five pitches, from treble to double bass, covering four octaves.

A *likembe* from Uganda and the Nyoro people is featured. The *likembe* is a hand instrument to which a number of metal or bamboo tongues are attached; the free ends of the tongues are plucked by two thumbs and first fingers, resulting in a sweet-toned sound. This instrument is also known as *mbira, kalimba* and *sansa.* Its name and construction vary from one part of Africa to another.

Chirombo Weye Nditerere is played on a *mbira* by Mugadzikwa Mwanagona, age thirteen, a Shona-Karanga boy from Rhodesia.

Musical bows, flutes, gourds, story songs, work songs and country dance songs are also featured.

Danses et Chants Bamoun. OCORA-SOR 3

"Musique Pour La Pendaison D'Un Ministre" features tuned drums. Record notes and photographs accompany this recording.

Drums of the Yoruba of Nigeria. Folkways—FE 4441

The Igbin drum selection includes two small drums playing a driving, interlocking, almost inseparable rhythm and a larger deep-toned drum playing intermittent rhythmic phrases.

Dundun is a pressure drum, played by professionals, and used for "talking." This recording presents a good illustration of talking drums playing drum phrases translated into Yoruba by another drummer.

Bata drums are also included. These are still played in Cuba.

The performance of Shango can be compared with Shango cult music of Latin America.

Ethiopie: Polyphonies et Techniques Vocales. OCORA-OCR 44

Among the various types of vocal music found in Ethiopia that are included in this recording are a canon sung by fifty men, an isochronic rhythm in parallel fifths, two young men singing two-part polyphony with one man singing a strictly repeated melodic formula (the other man has a different formula which he varies), an example of a melodic and verbal outline giving the impression of parallel seconds combined with a vibrato, and a selection where one man leads and is answered by a chorus which divides into two parts with one group sharply expelling their breath (giving the impression of roaring) while the second group alternates with the first, producing a basic rhythmic drone sung with vibrato.

In another equally valuable example one man leads and is accompanied by a chorus that alternates chest voice with falsetto in ascending glissando. Frequent interventions of whistling effects and of tense breath techniques are heard. Toward the end buzzing and falsetto vocal quality can be noticed.

Ewe Music of Ghana. AHM 4222

It is interesting to listen for the following Ewe bell pattern which is based on twelve even pulses:

It is found in several selections on this recording.

Folk Music of Ghana. Folkways—FW 8859

Band 5c on side 1 is a good example to compare with Latin American cult music.

The Tigari Cult Music has layers of sound which can be heard very clearly.

The use of work tools to produce musical sounds is illustrated in the second and third selections on the second side.

La Musique des Griots. OCORA-OCR 15

The *kora, gourdes frappées* and *khalam* or *halam* (which is similar to the banjo in sound and technique) can be heard on this recording.

Les Dogons. OCORA-OCR 33

Could accompany a study of Griaule's scholarly tome on the Dogon people.

Mbira Music of Rhodesia. University of Washington Press—UWP 1001

Included is a pamphlet written by the performer, Abraham Dumisani Maraire, which describes the background, composition and performance of *nyunga-nyunga mbira* music among the Shona people of Rhodesia.

Music from Rwanda. An Anthology of African Music (UNESCO Collection). Bärenreiter Musicaphone—BM 30L 2302

Includes performances on seven Tutsi *ngoma* or royal drums, the *inanga* (seven-stringed zither) and other instruments and types of music belonging to the Tutsi musical tradition.

The Music of the Dan. An Anthology of African Music (UNESCO Collection). Bärenreiter Musicaphone—BM 30L 2301

This useful recording of music in the Ivory Coast features festival music, drum rhythms, music for a chieftain, singing at a wrestling match, a sword-dance of the young girls, a *sanza* example, a song sung to encourage rice sowers, two small girls' singing games, rice harvest music, music for a mask race, music for the time when the mask Baegbo comes out (which features mirlitons or kazoo-like instruments), a trumpet orchestra, and a hunters song from the savannah and one from the forest.

The Music of the Diola. Folkways— FE 4323

A cultivating song, a pre-circumcision dance, and parade music performed during a circumcision fete are among the examples on this recording of the music of the Diola people of Senegal.

Music of the Jos Plateau and Other Regions of Nigeria. Folkways—FE 4321

Illustrates the variety of music cultures found in Nigeria. Found in the musical examples on this recording are variations of one melodic pattern, special whistles, interlocking patterns, banjo-like technique on a three-string Hausa lute, cattle horns used as instruments, gravel-like vocal quality, leader and response technique, and percussive use of instruments.

Music of the Mende of Sierra Leone. Folkways—FE 4322

Features a large bass *sanza* and a "talking" drum in the form of a slit gong. The *sanza* (or *sansa*) is a plucked idiophone found in many parts of Africa. A row of metal tongues of varying length are secured to a board, under which a calabash is fitted, which amplifies the sound of the plucked metal tongues. This instrument has many names including *mbira, kalimba* or *likembe,* depending upon the area of Africa in which it is found.

Music of the Princes of Dahomey. Counterpoint/Esoteric—537

Dahomean music is especially important since people from Dahomey are thought to have been brought in large numbers to the Americas. A lengthy segment of a Tohosson ceremony in Abomey, capital of the ancient kingdom of Dahomey, is included in this recording. The musical examples found most useful in the classroom are on side 2, bands 13 and 14, which consist of "vocalized" drum patterns.

Musique Baoule Kode. OCORA-OCR 34

Includes lengthy examples connected with the arrival, dance and leave-taking of a mask which give a sense of continuity that isolated examples may not have. This may be more useful for teachers than for students.

Musique D'Afrique Occidentale. Vogue—LVLX 193

Contains a good example of music played on a water drum and other drums. The following patterns are among those found in this music that students can easily hear and play.

The Hunter's dance has a fast, repeated scraper pattern which can be performed in class.

The dance that concludes the record employs different timbres in tight relationship to time but sporadic in their relationship to each other.

Musique Dahomeennes. OCORA-OCR 17

This recording is an important and useful resource for the classroom.

In the Nago (or Yoruba) music, the students can isolate and focus on each timbre and can perform with the *igba*.

In the Fon example, students can play with the metallophone, even using a stick and bottle, or with the rattles, using maracas.

See page 36 for a "score" of the Mahi example.

Musique du Burundi. OCORA-OCR 40

The whispered song is sung by one man accompanying himself on the *inanga*. This style of singing is not restricted to one singer, and it enables the performer to obtain a good balance between the voice and the *inanga*. This example becomes increasingly enjoyable with repeated hearings.

Songs accompanied by a musical bow, a *sanza* and an Akazehe greeting by two young girls are among the other examples found on this recording.

Musique du Cameroun. OCORA-OCR 25

These musical examples, recorded in different regions of the Cameroon, illustrate the diversity of musical styles found in this country. The unusually good quality of sound reproduction makes it easier to hear the different performers than in some recordings of African music. Side 2, band 6, is a good example for classroom use.

Musiques du Gabon. OCORA-OCR 41

Masango music, Fang xylophone and *mvet* (harp-zither) music, an Obamba walking song, Ndjabi music, Pounou music, Kota music and Pygmy music are included on this recording.

Musique Kabre du Nord—Togo. OCORA-OCR 16

Includes music played on xylophones and flutes, work songs, funeral music, hunting songs, and dances.

Musique Kongo. OCORA-OCR 35

An unusual recording that has several remarkably different examples that are important for those interested in African music.

A unique example is the Ba-Congo Musical Recreation song, sung by two Ba-Lari young women and accompanied by a combination of rattling percussion noises and sounds produced exclusively by the body, which include tongue-clicking sounds. The vocal vibrato is caused by striking the chin.

The Ba-Bembe horn ensemble uses four wooden horns, each carved from one piece of wood. The air column is located in that part of the instrument which is carved as a statue of a person; the mouthpiece is placed on the back between the shoulder blades.

There is a Ba-Lari Orchestra example utilizing a friction drum. Children's songs and lullabies also are included.

Musique Malgache. OCORA-OCR 24

Offers a wide variety of music, including examples of "slum" theater, from the island of Malagasy.

Musique Maure. OCORA-OCR 28

A well-documented recording, important for tracing certain sub-Saharan musical characteristics and their effect on southern Spanish (Andalusian) music.

The Naked Prey/African Music. Folkways—FS 3854

Features the N'Guni people and the sub-groups of Zulu and Xhosa. Try these patterns with the Zulu Boasting Song:

Fast six pulse (will not always be played on drums)

Negro Folk Music of Africa and America. Edited by Harold Courlander with Foreword by Richard Alan Waterman. Folkways—FE 4500

This collection provides a wealth of material for teachers making African/Afro-American comparisons. For example, the Music of the Boatmen from French Equatorial Africa uses stamping tubes which can be found in Haiti and Venezuela. Derivatives of Yoruba and Ibo (Nigeria) cultures can be found in Brazil, Haiti, Cuba and the United States. Examples are found on this recording from these and other cultures.

Niger: la Musique des Griots. OCORA-OCR 20

   An excellent recording for use in the classroom. Three examples that are particularly effective include music from the Ader people who live in Southern Niger and speak the Hausa language. This group of men sings to the accompaniment of large metal rings against which smaller metal rings are struck. Another example features Hausa people singing with long-necked lutes and rattles (see page 37 for a description of a classroom experience derived from this recording).

   Also included is a large Hausa ensemble of instruments playing music for the dead kings, which can be compared in instrumentation, tempo, mood and function with funeral music in New Orleans, e.g., "When the Saints Go Marching In."

Nigeria—Hausa Music I. An Anthology of African Music (UNESCO Collection). Bärenreiter Musicaphone—BM 30L 2306

   This excellent Hausa recording is worth having, for it shows the range found in that culture: butcher's rhythms, praise songs for blacksmiths, a praise song for farmers, fanfares for the Sultan of Sokoto and the Emir of Zaria, a song in praise of Nigeria and a song celebrating the investiture of the Emir of Kano.

Nigeria—Hausa Music II. An Anthology of African Music (UNESCO Collection). Bärenreiter Musicaphone—BM 30L 2307

   This recording continues to document the types of music found among the Hausa people. It is possible to get an idea of the range of music in an African culture through the study of these two recordings.

Nomades du Niger. OCORA-OCR 29

   Can assist teachers making a study of African influences in Spanish music. It is well documented.

The Pygmies of the Ituri Forest. Folkways—FE 4457

   Examples include musical characteristics found only in the music of the Pygmies. This recording features "hocketing" techniques, yodeling and the functional aspects of music in this culture.

Sounds of Africa. Verve—FTS 3021

   Highly recommended. Examples from all parts of the African continent are included, allowing the listener to hear how much the music varies from one part of Africa to another. The documentation prepared by Andrew Tracey is quite complete and very useful.

Tuareg Music of the Southern Sahara. Folkways—FE 4470

   Particularly helpful for teachers studying the African influence on

Andalusian music and the music of Latin America. It is an excellent recording with good documentation.

Valiha: Madagascar. OCORA-OCR 18

The *valiha* is a fairly long, tubular instrument with strings that are held away from the surface of the instrument by small bridges. The *valiha* is held in the palms of the hands and plucked with the fingers, producing an extremely pleasing sound.

Wolof Music of Senegal and Gambia. Folkways—FE 4462

Several examples are included of the *halam,* which is believed by some authorities to be the progenitor of the banjo.

Discontinued Recordings

The following recordings are no longer issued, but may be found in record libraries or in the personal collections of persons who have traveled in Africa. Because they are excellent recordings, they have been included in this Source Book.

African Dances of the Witwatersrand Gold Mines (Part 1). Hugh Tracey. Decca—LF 1254

Features the dancing of the Chopi people of Mozambique. In the Mutshongolo stamping dance of the Shangaan people, the performers often strike their shields with their sticks to punctuate a dance action.

African Dances of the Witwatersrand Gold Mines (Part 2). Hugh Tracey. Decca—LF 1255

An excellent recording that includes a Muchongolo tumbling dance of the Ndau people from the Mpanda district of Mozambique; a Umteyo shaking dance of Xhosa people from the Ciskei, Cape Province, South Africa (incorporates the sound of leg rattles and small bells strapped across the chests of the dancers); the Mohobelo striding dance of the Southern Sotho people from Basutoland, with stamping and hissing; and the famous Isicathulo gumboot dance of the Baca people from Cape Province.

African Music Society's Choice. Best Recordings for 1953 (Part 1). Hugh Tracey. Decca—LF 1224

This excellent recording features "Kokoro" (or Benjamin Aderounmu), a blind Yoruba, accompanying himself on his drum in Lagos, Nigeria.

In one example, twelve *entenga* drums of the Banda of Mengo, Uganda, are played by the royal drummers. The parts are first played alone, then combined, so they can better be understood.

African Music Society's Best Music for 1952. Hugh Tracey. Decca—LF 1171
Among the examples on this recording are a Kathandi *mbira* accompanying a song about a train and a Tutsi boy and his father who sing a chief's song, illustrating Tutsi chanting.

Drums of East Africa. Music of Africa Series. Hugh Tracey. Decca—LF 1120
Features five Enkoito drums of the Nyoro Haya people.
Side 2 consists of fourteen Tutsi drum rhythms from Rwanda.

The Guitars of Africa. Music of Africa Series. Hugh Tracey. Decca—LF 1170
An excellent recording featuring a variety of guitar styles.

CLASSROOM EXPERIENCES

To comprehend many types of black music, musicians need to reexamine their techniques of listening, for some black music does not yield easily to listening habits which are biased in favor of a theme-harmony sensitivity.

Because of the importance of vertical pitch organization in musical styles most familiar to us, we listen with a broad focus to the harmony that supports a theme or motive. We know that harmony results from the combining of layers of single, pitched lines. However, we tend not to isolate and examine one apart from the others, favoring a perception of blocks of sound, rather than separate linear strands. We apprehend more the *resultant effect* of the combined lines, rather than the separate lines themselves. We use these listening techniques even when the music we hear is based on different textural processes (as is much black music). In addition, we are often insensitive to the rhythmic element in black music because of our concentration on this theme-harmony orientation.

The experiences that follow are intended to develop a greater awareness of sound as it occurs in time. We are encouraging students to create music to help them increase their understanding of how it is organized and how the elements of music interact. Teachers should view these classroom experiences not as rigid lesson plans but as a source of ideas for using many of the materials listed in this Source Book.

Each experience is followed by one or more experiments designed to fulfill the stated purpose. Each experiment must be kept moving to be effective. Students should be encouraged to contribute ideas for related experiments.

Experience I.
Focusing the ear to follow separate layers of sound.

Have students use their hands to assist their ears in focusing on two layers of sound. The sound source could be footsteps.

Appoint four students, in different areas of the room, to walk back and forth as you point to one or two of them. The other students should close their eyes. As students begin to walk, ask them to point to the source of the sound of the footsteps. Occasionally start one student while another is walking so that two lines of sound must be pointed to by the students. Try varying the loudness and tempo of the footsteps. Ask a student to conduct the four students. Try this experiment with instruments, radios, tape recorded material or voices.

Experience II.

Assisting the ear to perceive several different layers of sound when only one layer is heard.

Make several tape loops, each containing one phrase spoken by a student. For example, Steve Reich's composition entitled "Come Out" *(Music in Our Time.* Odyssey—32-16-0160) makes use of the phrase "Come out to show them." As this phrase repeats, the students should begin to lose the sense of a voice speaking and begin to hear it as an "instrumental" timbre.

Ask students to hear rhythmic patterns created by listening to different combinations of the words. For example, ask them to respond to the rhythmic pattern created by isolating aurally the first two words, as: "come out . . . come out . . . come out"; then "to show . . . come."

Observe other combinations of words and resultant rhythm patterns; for example, the last word in combination with the second, or feeling the last word as a downbeat or accented beat. Experiments may incorporate loops of the same material with silence added so that the two loops are slightly out-of-phase, or may combine loops with other verbal material of varying lengths.

This experiment is similar to listening to an unaccompanied Bach cello sonata in that one hears certain pitches in a single line assuming both melodic and harmonic functions.

Students perceive new layers of sound as they focus their ears on different combinations of words (or notes if the experiment is tried with a single layer of pitches), rather than perceiving only the explicit intentions of the composer. This is more like the kind of listening practiced in some parts of Africa.

Experience III.

Becoming more aware of time in which sound is placed in order to create music.

Have the students note the time that elapses between presentations of different timbres in several musical examples. They will need a second hand on a clock or watch.

For example, note the similarities when comparing the elapsed time between changes in timbre in an African example, an electronic music example, a movement of a classical symphony and a piece of popular music. In music of different styles, the rate in appearance of new timbres evokes a sense of time.

Listening for timbral changes involves extreme sensitivity to minute fluctuations in sound quality. This sensitivity can be developed by means of experiments dealing with changes in volume, texture, location of sound sources in the classroom and timbres resulting from combinations of sounds. This sensitivity is extremely important in studying black music.

Experience IV.

Experimenting with a moveable downbeat or accent to expand a uniform metrical feeling of sound in time.

Divide the class in half. Have one-half clap: 1 – 3 – while the other half claps: – 2 – 4. The students should count aloud as they clap.

Encourage them to note the tendency of the 2 and 4 to become uncertain, slower or less aggressive.

Ask them to listen to the result when both groups believe they are clapping on 1 and 3.

Part 1:   1 — 3 —
Part 2:   — 1 — 3

Students clapping Part 2 should feel more aggressive and certain as they think of the pattern as 1 and 3 instead of 2 and 4. They might feel this because they believe they are on and not off the beat.

Now, ask the students to clap eight even pulses. Have them repeat this, accenting the first in each series of eight claps.

Divide the class into 5 sections. Have the first section begin with the others entering as follows, repeating continuously until all sections have entered and students have heard the results.

Section 1:	1	2	3	4	5	6	7	8				
Section 2:		1	2	3	4	5	6	7	8			
Section 3:			1	2	3	4	5	6	7	8		
Section 4:				1	2	3	4	5	6	7	8	
Section 5:					1	2	3	4	5	6	7	8

Psychologically, we appear to treat "weaker" beats such as 2 and 4 as *reactions* to accented beats. Perhaps not all cultures feel this way. Experimenting with our reactions through such exercises may assist us to understand the different functions an accented beat can perform. It also alerts us to possibilities which might be employed in music of other cultures.

Experience V.

Continuing to experiment with breaking out of a uniformly conceived metrical structure.

Have the students think of a note and sing that note on "ah" when you cue them. A dense cluster, or pitch conglomerate, will result.

From the available pitches, select three pitches (as C, D and E). Have the students sing or play them together until a meter of 3 is generated.

Next, divide the class into three groups and have the students sing or play those pitches (numbered 1 – 2 – 3), entering as follows, repeating continuously:

```
Group 1:  1   2   3
Group 2:      1   2   3
Group 3:          1   2   3
```

As you, or a student, hold up one, two or three fingers, ask the students to stress the number which corresponds to the fingers being held up. Do this until the students can feel the different sense of time being generated by the changes in stress.

Experience VI.

Developing a "metronome sense" which seems to be an important ingredient of African music.

Put these numbers on the board to be used as symbols for the sounds students will make.

1   2   3   4   5   6   7   8

Have the students clap when you point to 1. If they are not together, ask them to do it again. Urge them to clap fairly lightly.

Count "1-2-3-4-5-6-7-go" and point to each number as they clap. Have them do this again, getting a clean sound on each clap. Once more, ask them to clap all eight, with a good attack on each one, but very quietly and evenly.

If their tempo increases, take a few minutes to have them clap once every second, if there is a second hand on the clock, or each time you lower your hand, so that they experience again the control of tempo. Perhaps it will help if you quietly say "Relax your shoulders" or "Breathe freely."

Put these numbers on the board:

1   2   3   4   **5**   6   7   8

Ask them to clap more loudly on the ones which are bolder. Here are some additional examples:

1	2	**3**	4	**5**	6	**7**	8
1	2	3	**4**	5	6	**7**	8
1	2	**3**	4	**5**	6	7	8
1	2	3	**4**	5	6	7	8
1	**2**	3	4	**5**	**6**	7	8
1	2	**3**	4	5	**6**	7	8

Try these in different combinations, with some students playing on desks.

Clap loudly on the following bold numbers; hit the desk or knee on the lighter numbers.

1	2	**3**	4	**5**	6	7	8
1	2	**3**	4	**5**	6	**7**	8
1	**2**	3	4	**5**	6	7	8
1	2	**3**	**4**	5	6	**7**	**8**

Repeat the following patterns, clapping only on the bold numbers while hitting the air on the lighter numbers. Counting should be encouraged.

1	2	**3**	**4**	5	6	**7**	8
1	2	**3**	4	**5**	6	7	8

Gradually increase tempo until each pattern is quite brisk.

Have the students play both of these lines, one after the other, clapping only on the bold numbers and hitting the air on the lighter numbers. Repeat them continuously several times until the students feel the patterns and can stay together without counting aloud.

1	2	3	**4**	5	6	**7**	8
1	2	**3**	4	**5**	6	7	8

Ask one student to count loudly while the class combines the above patterns, then with the four patterns below, use a variety of hand positions or instruments to create differences in timbre. The students should continue to do this until they are no longer counting numbers but are reproducing a rhythmic pattern with which they are completely at ease.

1	2	**3**	4	**5**	6	**7**	8
1	2	**3**	4	**5**	6	**7**	8
1	**2**	3	4	**5**	**6**	7	8
1	2	**3**	**4**	5	6	**7**	**8**

Have the students again experience putting several patterns together. Start by putting these numbers on the board:

1	2	3	4	5	6

Have the students clap each of them, then clap on 1 – 3 – 5, then 1 – 4, as below:

1   2   **3**   4   **5**   6
1   2   3   **4**   5   6

Create many combinations of 6, 8 and 12 pulses. Have the students perform these patterns with recordings of popular Afro-American, Brazilian, Latin American music and rock.

Encourage the students to make up their own patterns as a class, in small groups or as individuals. The pulse upon which the patterns should be based is provided in the recorded music. This pulse framework can be felt in half or double time. For example, the students might consider a ¼ measure containing all eight pulses upon which their pattern is based. However, they might be more comfortable using two measures of ¼, making their pulses match the strong beats of each measure (1 and 3). Some students will want to challenge their virtuosity by feeling their pattern of eight pulses in the first half of one measure of ¼.

Students should be led to feel these patterns, gradually moving from counting aloud to reacting internally to the underlying pulse. Patterns can be formed which are of different lengths, yet steady in relation to the pulse on which they are based.

Experience VII.

Experiencing cross-rhythms using two against three.

Much African and Afro-American music makes use of a rhythmic feeling of two against three. Students should be able to feel it almost automatically. The following steps are suggested to accomplish this. These steps may be undertaken on successive days.

Put on the chalkboard:

LEFT		RIGHT
1	1	1
	2	
	3	3
	4	
	5	5
	6	

Have the students raise their hands and strike the first pulse with both hands on an imaginary wall in front of them as a student counts to 6 aloud.

Then have them tap 1, 3 and 5 with the right hand. Repeat this at a reasonable speed until it is set.

Put this on the board:

LEFT		RIGHT
1	1	1
	2	
	3	
4	4	
	5	
	6	

Have the students play 1 again with both hands, and 1 – 4 with their left hand. Repeat this example until it is set.

Have the students combine the two, putting the following on the board:

	LEFT		RIGHT	
	1	1	1	
		2		
TWO		3	3	THREE
BEATS	4	4		BEATS
		5	5	
		6		

After they have done this combined exercise until it is fluent, change the numbers as follows to illustrate that they are playing two beats with the left hand while playing three with the right hand.

L	R
1	1
•	•
•	2
2	•
•	3
•	•

Have them count aloud the beats played by the right hand (1 – 2 – 3), then the left hand (1 – 2), while keeping both hands going. Repeat this process until they can keep both hands going while they change counts.

Do not count for this step. Start the students on the left/right pattern without counting aloud. Have them lower their hands onto their desks or thighs while they are playing the pattern. Insist on precision in the pattern, avoiding the tendency to rush.

Individuals in our culture often equate ability with speed. In this experiment such an attitude must be avoided.

Have the students play loudly with one hand and softly with the other. This presents a coordination problem which they will soon solve. Ask them to continue playing the pattern with both hands while they move first one hand and then the other off their desk. The resultant sound should involve a smooth change from 2 to 3. Repeat this until it can be done easily and at several tempos.

Recordings listed in the discography which contain examples of two against three:

Nigeria—Hausa Music I (See page 25). Side 1, band 6
Drums of East Africa (See page 27). Side 1, band 2
Musiques du Gabon (See page 23). Side 1, band 2
Music from Rwanda (See page 21). Side 2, band 11; side 2, band 15
Niger: la Musique des Griots (See page 25). Side 1, band 7

Experience VIII.

Additional work with patterns based on a continuous pulse.

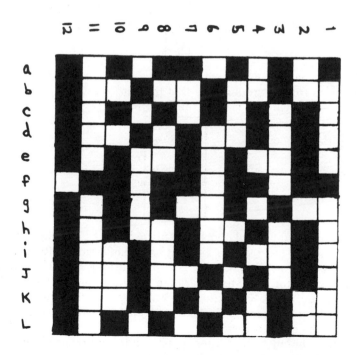

This "crossword puzzle" has twelve equal-size squares, each of which is considered to be a pulse. Students can use any timbre or pitch and play the patterns made by the white squares or the black squares, going in any direction. In fact, they can play parts of the patterns—beginning, middle or end. Most students are capable of making up their own rhythm patterns; however, this experience can serve to stimulate rhythmic ideas.

Experience IX.

Listening with scores to examples of African music to assist in focusing the ear.

In transcribing African music, one runs the terrible risk of totally misrepresenting the music. These examples are scored with as much care as possible and are not to be construed as precise depictions of what the performers on the recording are visualizing or hearing. They are meant to be of assistance to American students. Each score represents only a suggestion of the actual music.

Example A: Yoruba Drummers From Nigeria. *Sounds of Africa.* Verve— FTS 3021 (see page 25). Side 1, band 1

This very short example, an excerpt from a Yoruba folk opera, exhibits the precision of the drummers of the Yoruba people, who live in western Nigeria. The students would benefit from this example if they would try to play part of it before they hear it. The patterns below are played one after the other, then repeated.

Low-pitched drum:
(H = high
L = low
M = medium)

1	•	3	•	5	•	•	•	9	10	11	•
L		L		L				H	H	H	
1	•	•	4	•	•	7	•	9	10	11	•
L			L			Rim		H	H	H	

Dry sound:

•	•	3	•	5	•	7	•	•	10	•	•
		H		L		M			M		
1	•	•	•	•	•	•	•	9	•	11	•
M								M		M	
1	•	•	4	•	•	7	•	•	10	•	•
M			M			M			M		
1	•	3	•	5	•	7	•	•	•	•	•
M		M		M		M					

High-pitched drum:

•	•	3	•	5	•	7	•	•	10	•	•
1	•	3	•	•	6	•	•	9	•	•	•
1	•	3	•	5	•	•	•	9	•	•	•
1	•	3	•	•	•	7	•	•	•	•	•

Example B: "Toba" from the Mahi people of Dahomey. *Musique Dahomeennes.* OCORA-OCR 17 (see page 23). Side 1, band 1

This score may look confusing but after hearing the musical example it will become obvious how it assists the ear to focus on what the instruments are doing. Students may be able to perform this piece with or without recording.

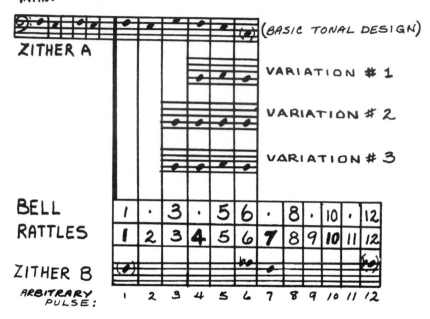

Example C: *Danses et Chants Bamoun.* OCORA-SOR 3 (see page 19). Side 1, band 1

Have the students learn this piece from the score, following the numbered patterns based on nine even pulses. This selection should be played quite slowly and with dignity.

Suggested Procedure:
1. Learn A.
2. Listen to recording and quietly tap A.
3. Learn A and B variations.
4. Listen to recording and indicate when A and B variations are heard.
5. Perform music without record.

Score:

A Pitches:

	1	2	3	4	5	6	7	8	9
d'	1	2	3	•	5	6	•	8	•
c'	•	•	•	•	•	•	7	•	•
a	•	•	•	•	•	•	•	•	9

A Variations (occasionally omit numbers in parentheses)

Pitches:

	1	2	3	4	5	6	7	8	9
d'	1	(2)	3	•	5	(6)	•	(8)	•
c'	•	•	•	(4)	•	•	7	•	•
a	•	•	•	•	•	(6)	•	•	9

B Pitches:

	1	2	3	4	5	6	7	8	9
d'	1	2	3	•	5	•	7	8	9
c'	•	•	•	4	•	•	•	•	•
a	•	•	•	•	•	6	•	•	•

	1	2	3	4	5	6	7	8	9
Medium high drum (unchanging)	1	•	•	4	•	•	7	•	•
Medium low drum	•	•	•	•	•	•	7	8	9
Low octave of the one above	1	•	3	4	•	•	•	•	•
Brushed sound	•	2	•	4	•	(6)	•	8	9

Section A is used almost all the time. Section B and the variations occasionally can be alternated with Section A.

Example D: "Bako" performed by the Hausa people of the Republic of Niger. *Niger: la Musique des Griots.* OCORA-OCR 20. (See page 25). Side 2, band 2

This example of voices, long-necked lutes and rattles from the Republic of Niger can be performed with the recording. Here are two patterns, the first of which is the rhythm of the long-necked lutes. The second pattern is that of the rattles. Performing these while listening to the voices allows students to feel the rhythmic characteristics of the piece.

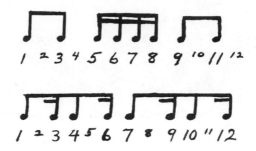

Experience X.
Performing percussion pieces from scores.

The following scores are presented for use in whatever ways may seem appropriate (H=high, L=low, M=medium):

SCORE NO. 1

	1	2	3	4	5	6	7	8
Master drum	1	•	•	4	5	•	•	•
High drum	•	•	•	•	•	•	7	8
Medium drum	•	2	3	•	•	6	•	•
Clap	1	•	3	4	5	•	7	8
Two-tone bell	1 H	2 H	3 L	4 H	5 H	•	•	•
Woodblock	1 1	• 2	3 •	• 4	5 •	• 6	7 •	• 8
Rattle	1 • •	• 2 •	• • 3	4 • •	• 5 •	• • 6	7 • •	• 8 •

SCORE NO. 2

	1	2	3	4	5	6	7	8
Medium low drum I	1	•	3	•	5	6	•	8
	•	2	•	4	5	6	7	•
Medium drum	1	•	3	•	5	•	7	•
	•	2	3	•	5	6	•	•
Master drum	1	•	•	•	5	•	7	•
	L	•	•	•	H	•	H	•
	1	•	•	•	5	•	•	•
	L	•	•	•	H	•	•	•
Low drum	1	•	•	•	5	•	7	•
	H	•	•	•	H	•	L	•
	1	•	•	4	•	•	7	•
Medium high drum I	•	2	•	•	5	•	•	8
	•	•	3	•	•	6	•	•
Medium high drum II	1	•	•	4	•	•	•	•
High drum	1	2	•	•	5	6	•	•
	1	•	•	4	5	•	•	•
Medium low drum II	•	•	•	4	5	•	•	•
Rattle	1	2	3	4	5	6	7	8
One-tone bell	1	•	•	4	5	•	•	8
Guiro	1	•	3	•	5	•	7	•
	1	•	•	4	5	•	7	•
Woodblock	1	•	•	4	•	•	•	•
	1	•	3	•	5	•	7	•

39

SCORE NO. 3

	1	2	3	4	5	6	7	8
Master drum	1	•	3	4	5	•	7	8
	1	•	3	4	5	•	7	•
Low drum I	1	2	•	•	•	•	7	8
	•	•	•	•	5	•	7	•
Medium high drum	•	2	3	•	5	6	•	8
Medium low drum I	1	•	•	•	•	•	7	•
	•	•	•	4	•	•	•	•
Medium low drum II	•	•	•	4	•	•	•	•
	1	•	•	•	•	•	7	•
High drum	1	•	•	•	•	•	•	•
	•	•	•	•	•	•	7	•
Rattle	•	•	3	•	•	•	•	•
Medium drum	1	•	•	4	•	•	7	•
Small woodblock	1	•	•	4	•	•	•	•
Low drum II	1	•	•	4	•	•	7	•
	•	2	•	•	5	•	•	•
Large woodblock	1	•	3	•	5	•	7	•

SCORE NO. 4

(U = up D = down)	1	2	3	4	5	6	7	8	9	10	11	12
Master drum	1	•	3	4	•	6	7	•	9	10	•	12
Low drum	1	•	•	4	•	6	7	•	•	10	•	12
Medium low drum	1	•	3	•	5	6	7	•	•	10	•	12
Low drum	1	•	•	4	•	•	7	•	•	10	•	•
Medium drum	•	2	•	4	•	6	•	8	•	10	•	12
High drum	1	2	3	4	5	6	7	8	9	10	11	12
	H	L	H	H	L	H	H	L	H	H	L	H
Medium high drum	•	2	3	•	5	6	•	8	9	•	11	12
Medium low drum	1	2	3	4	5	6	7	8	9	10	11	12
	L	L	H	L	L	H	L	L	H	L	L	H
Two-tone bell	1	•	3	•	5	6	•	8	•	10	•	12
	L	•	H	•	H	H	•	H	•	H	•	H
Large woodblock	1	•	3	•	5	•	7	•	9	•	11	•
Rattle	1	•	3	4	5	6	7	8	9	10	11	12
	U	•	D	U	D	D	U	D	U	D	U	D
Sung 5th of major scale	•	•	•	•	5	6	•	•	•	•	11	•
					Ya	- ku					- ku	
Sung 3rd of major scale	•	•	•	•	•	•	7	8	9	10	•	•
							Ke	- le	- le	Ya -		

Experience XI.
Developing ideas for improvisation from musical examples.

There is one primary rule in improvisation:

Anything is allowed in improvisation as long as it does not disrupt the context or the framework of which the improvisation is a part. Silence as well as sound should be incorporated.

One way to be sure it will not be disruptive is to make the improvisation gradual. If it begins with the improvisor performing comfortably as part of the established texture, it will be more successful, because the character of the piece will set itself in the improvisor's mind and disruptive improvisation will be minimized.

The purpose for the inclusion of Afro-American music in the following experiment is to assist in the student's transition from musical functions that are more familiar to those derived from an African context.

These examples should be used in ways that are effective for the students, and the ideas should be withheld if they stifle musical thought. Let the music generate ideas for student improvisation. It is intended that these recordings be listened to in the order presented.

1. *Music of the Dan.* Bärenreiter—BM 30L 2301. Side 2, band 10 (see page 21).

     Illustrates an approach to improvisation whereby each part fits in with that which is already played.

2. *Batucada Fantastica.* MGM—E/SE 4085. Side 1, bands 2 and 3.
     Two pieces for percussion in which each part enters separately.

3. *Mother Nature's Son.* Ramsey Lewis. Cadet—LPS-821.
     Examples of different timbres and new improvised patterns.

4. *Soul Bag.* Mongo Santamaria. Columbia—CS 9653. "Chili Beans." Side 2, band 6.

     Use of a constant rhythmic pattern; note rhythmic relationships between the entrances of the piano and trumpet parts.

     Piano pattern (8 pulses):   1   •   •   4   •   •   7   •
                                  •   •   3   •   5   •   •   •

5. *Musiques du Cameroun.* OCORA-OCR 25. Side 2, band 3 (see page 23).
     Rather clear parts, to be used as a foundation for improvisation.

6. *Ain't It Funky?* James Brown. King—KS 1092. Side 1, band 1.
     Simple rhythmic texture with variations; repetition as a device to provide security for improvisation.

7. *Elis.* Companhia Brasileira de Discos—P 765.001 P. "Roda." Side 1, band 1.

     Very precise performance of set patterns alternating after a short silence with a steady beat pattern in unison.

8. *Music from Rwanda.* Bärenreiter—BM 30L 2302. Side 1, band 1 (see page 21).

     Almost unison performance of patterns based on a continuous pulse, with drummers taking turns stressing certain pulses to throw the rhythmic feeling into different frameworks.

9. *Drums of East Africa.* Decca—LF 1120. Side 1, band 4 (see page 27).

Ganda drummers from Uganda start with sticks on the side of the drum; then, one by one, they play their patterns using the drum heads. They then play all together returning to sticks on the side of the drum, and conclude by playing the rhythm on the drum heads.

Note how their patterns interlock to create a "bubbling" texture. Experiment with this effect through improvisation.

10. *Music of the Princes of Dahomey.* Counterpoint/Esoteric—537. Side 2, bands 13 and 14 (see page 22).

Note how these two princes from Dahomey "vocalize" their drum patterns. Try to improvise a pattern which is based on "interior" or sounded vocalization. You can make up your own.

Example: Da keeta keeta
Da deng deng deng
Da keeta keeta
Da deng – – – – –
or
Kong kong kadong
Kong kong kong kadong

11. *Nigeria—Hausa Music 1.* Bärenreiter Musicaphone—BM 30L 2306. Side 2, band 10 (see page 25).

Establish a pulse, then take turns playing short solos while the rest keep the pulse going.

12. *Musique Kongo.* OCORA-OCR 35. Side 2, bands 2 and 3 (see page 23).

Sporadic use of different timbres.

13. *Nara Pede Passagem.* Companhia Brasileira de Discos—P 632.787 L. Side 1, band 1.

Accompany a song on this recording by adding patterns one at a time.

14. *Nara Pede Passagem.* Companhia Brasileira de Discos—P 632.787 L. Side 1, band 4.

Improvise a pattern and add a simple, repeated vocal pattern.

15. *Roots of the Blues.* Atlantic 1348. "Train Time." Side 2, band 4.

Improvise patterns which can be interspersed with reading, speaking, singing or playing an instrument.

16. *African Concert.* Philips—PCC 214. Side 1, band 5.

A short example of "talking drums," a drum message from the Congo. It would be helpful to read about talking drums (see page 18).

Construct a piece which consists of uneven phrases using high and low pitch register areas.

17. *Batucada No. 2.* Companhia Brasileira de Discos—P 632.180 L. Side 1, band 5.

    These are two Macumba (cult) rhythms from Brazil. Notice the careful use of different timbres.

18. *Batucada Fantastica.* MGM—E/SE 4085. Side 1, band 1.

    Try improvising a piece which allows each instrument to play its part alone between sections where everyone plays.

19. *Africa South of the Sahara.* Folkways—FE 503. Side 4, band 36 (see page 17).

    If you want students to play along with the music, do not begin patterns until the bell enters; this pattern is longer, and the second half of it does not start on one.

    Bell   1 • 3 4 • 6 • 8 • 10 • 12
    Clap   • 2 • 4 5 • 7 • 9 • 11 •

    This is a continuous cycle. Play one line after the other and repeat. The bell enters on beat 1. Slowing the speed at first may be necessary to cope with this example. The stamping heard in the background is on these pulses:

    1 • • 4 • • 7 • • 10 • •

20. *Batucada Fantastica.* MGM—E/SE 4085. Side 1, band 6.

    Try an improvisation with only four parts, forming several small groups.

22. *Batucada Fantastica.* MGM—E/SE 4085. Side 1, band 10.

    An improvisation can use a wide range of pitch areas; also it is interesting to have them interrupted by a different timbre.

23. *Batucada Fantastica.* MGM—E/SE 4085. Side 2, band 1.

    The following four examples are Candomblé (cult) rhythms from Brazil. Use them as you like.

24. *Drums of East Africa.* Decca—LF 1120. Side 2 (see page 27).

    These are fourteen different rhythmic patterns played by the Watutsi Mwami's (king's) royal drummers. The first is called "Umusuko." The rest will be announced by a man's voice.

PART II

Afro-American Music

PART II

BIBLIOGRAPHY

Books on Afro-Americans

Commentaries

The following books are historical, sociological, psychological and literary commentaries on Afro-Americans. Representative samples from this list should be read by music educators who want to broaden their perspective on American culture.

Adler, M. J. *et al.* (ed.). *The Negro in American History.* 3 volumes. Chicago: Encyclopedia Britannica Educational Corporation, 1969.
> Significant source material to help the reader relate the contributions of the black man to American life and culture. Private diaries and letters, selected statements, editorials, opinions, court decisions, poetry and songs are included.

Alexander, Rae Pace (compiler). *Young and Black in America.* New York: Random House, 1970. Introductory notes by Julius Lester.
> A compilation of excerpts from books by eight black Americans. The excerpts give evidence of the oppression and racism the authors suffered as children and young adults.

Aptheker, Herbert. *A Documentary History of the Negro People in the United States.* 2 volumes. New York: Citadel, 1951.
> Readable selections from a wide variety of sources. Volume I covers the period through the Civil War; Volume II, from Reconstruction to 1910.

Baldwin, James. *The Fire Next Time.* New York: The Dial Press, 1963, or New York: Dell, 1970.

Bennett, Lerone, Jr. *Before the Mayflower: A History of the Negro in America, 1619-1964.* Revised edition. Baltimore: Pelican Books, 1966.
> A popularized history, based on a series of articles published in Ebony magazine.

Bennett, Lerone, Jr. *The Negro Mood.* Chicago: Johnson Publishing Company, 1964, or New York: Barnes and Noble, Inc., 1970.

Bergman, Peter M. *The Chronological History of the Negro in America.* New York: Harper & Row, 1969.

This handbook presents a prose account of selected facts, organized annually from 1492-1968, highlighting the history of the Negro in America. Bibliographical references and an index with chronological references conclude the book.

Brown, Claude. *Manchild in the Promised Land.* New York: Signet Books, 1966.

Cleaver, Eldridge. *Soul on Ice.* New York: McGraw-Hill, 1967.

Congress on Africa: Africa and the American Negro. Miami: Mnemosyne Publishing Co., Inc., 1969.

Culp, D. W. (ed.). *Twentieth Century Negro Literature.* New York: Arno Press, 1969.

Curtin, Phillip. *The Atlantic Slave Trade.* Madison, Wisconsin: University of Wisconsin Press, 1969.

A concise record of the slave trade, with documentation.

Dodds, B. *Negro Literature for High School Students.* Champaign, Illinois: National Council of Teachers of English, 1968.

Dorson, Richard M. (collector). *American Negro Folktales.* Greenwich, Connecticut: Fawcett Premier Book, 1968.

Douglass, Frederick. *The Narrative of the Life of Frederick Douglass.* Boston: 1854. New York: Doubleday & Co., Inc., 1969.

Douglass discusses his life and times. His writing is colored by the oratorical rhetoric of the first half of the nineteenth century but has a style that is cogent and disarmingly direct.

Dover, Cedric. *American Negro Art.* Greenwich, Connecticut: New York Graphic Society, 1960.

A survey of the black American's contribution to art from colonial times to the present. Includes numerous illustrations.

Drotning, P. T. *Guide to Negro History in America.* New York: Doubleday & Co., Inc., 1968.

Dubois, W. E. B. *The Souls of Black Folk.* Greenwich, Connecticut: Signet Books, 1903 (Reprinted, 1969).

Fishel, Leslie II. and Benjamin Quarles. *The Negro American: A Documentary History.* New York: William Morrow & Co., Inc., 1967.

Franklin, John Hope. *From Slavery to Freedom: A History of Negro Americans.* Third edition, revised. New York: Alfred A. Knopf, Inc., 1967.

Frazier, E. F. *The Negro in the United States.* New York: Macmillan, 1957.

Gayle, Addison, Jr. *The Black Aesthetic.* Garden City: Doubleday and Company, 1971.
An anthology of thirty-four articles discussing the function and responsibilities of the black artist (musician, poet, dramatist and author).

Goldston, Robert. *The Negro Revolution: From Its African Genesis to the Death of Martin Luther King.* New York: Macmillan, 1968.

Gottleib, David and Anne L. Heinsohn. *America's Other Youth: Growing Up Poor.* Englewood Cliffs, New Jersey: Prentice-Hall, 1971.

Grier, W. H. and P. M. Cobbs. *Black Rage.* New York: Basic Books, Inc., 1968.

Herndon, James. *The Way It Spozed to Be.* New York: Bantam Books, 1969.
Provides a graphic description of teaching in a black ghetto school.

Herskovits, Melville J. *The Myth of the Negro Past.* Boston: Beacon Press, 1958.
An anthropological study tracing black Americans' attitudes and cultural characteristics to their African antecedents.

Herskovits, Melville J. *The New World Negro: Selected Papers in Afro-American Studies.* New York: Funk and Wagnalls Co., 1969.

Herskovits, Melville J. *Suriname Folk-Lore.* New York: A M S Press, Inc., 1969.

Hoover, D. W. (ed.). *Understanding Negro History.* Chicago: Quadrangle Books, Inc., 1969.

Hughes, Langston. *New Negro Poets: U.S.A.* Bloomington: Indiana University Press, 1964.

Hughes, Langston and Arna Bontemps. *Book of Negro Folklore.* New York: Dodd, Mead & Co., 1958.

Hughes, Langston and Milton Meltzer. *Black Magic: A Pictorial History of the Negro in American Entertainment.* Englewood Cliffs, New Jersey: Prentice-Hall, 1967.

Hughes, Langston and Milton Meltzer. *Pictorial History of the Negro in America.* New York: Crown Publishers, Inc., 1968.

Interesting Memoirs and Documents Relating to American Slavery and the Glorious Struggle Now Making for Complete Emancipation. Miami: Mnemosyne Publishing Co., Inc., 1969.

Jahn, Janheinz. *History of Neo-African Literature: Writing in Two Continents.* London: Faber & Faber, Ltd., 1968.

Jones, L. and L. Neal (eds.). *Black Fire: An Anthology of Afro-American Writing.* New York: William Morrow & Co., 1968.

Katz, Bernard (ed.). *Social Implications of Early American Negro Music.* New York: Arno Press, 1969.

King, Martin Luther, Jr. *Where Do We Go From Here: Chaos or Community.* Boston: Beacon Press, Inc., 1968.

Lee, Ulysses, William Loren Katz, *et al. The American Negro: History and Literature,* Series 1, 2 and 3 (140 volumes). New York: Arno Press/The New York Times.

Lesson Plans on African-American History. Compiled, written and edited by New York City teachers. New York: United Federation of Teachers, 1969.

Lester, Julius. *Black Folktales.* New York: Richard W. Baron Publishing Co., Inc., 1969.

Lincoln, C. Eric. *The Negro Pilgrimage in America.* New York: Bantam Books, 1967.

Malcolm X. *The Autobiography of Malcolm X.* With Alex Haley. New York: Grove Press, Inc., 1964.

Mannix, Daniel Pratt and Malcolm Cowley. *Black Cargoes.* New York: Viking Press, 1962.
    A readable, interesting discussion of the slave trade, with illustrations and bibliography.

Meltzer, Milton (ed.). *In Their Own Words: A History of the American Negro.* 3 volumes. New York: Thomas Y. Crowell Company, 1965.

Parks, Gordon. *Born Black.* Philadelphia: J. B. Lippincott Co., 1971.

Piro, Richard. *Black Fiddler.* New York: William Morrow & Co., Inc., 1971.
    A teacher's description of a school production of "Fiddler on the Roof."

Redding, Saunders. *They Came in Chains: Americans from Africa.* Philadelphia: J. B. Lippincott Co., 1950.

 Surveys black history from colonial times to the Truman administration.

Schoener, Allen. *Harlem on My Mind: Cultural Capital of Black America, 1900-1968.* New York: Random House, 1969.

 Harlem's daily life as well as the artistic and literary leaders it has produced are documented by this collection of photographs that were first shown at a Metropolitan Museum of Art exhibition in 1967.

Silberman, Charles E. *Crisis in Black and White.* New York: Vintage Books, 1964.

Smith-Bowen, Elenore. *Return to Laughter.* Garden City, New York: Anchor Book, Doubleday & Co., 1954.

Washington, Joseph R. *Black Religion.* Boston: Beacon Press, 1964.

Whitten, Norman E., Jr. and John F. Szwed. *Afro-American Anthropology: Contemporary Perspectives.* New York: Free Press, 1970.

Woodson, Carter G. and Charles Wesley. *The Negro in Our History.* 10th edition revised. Washington, D.C.: Associated Publishers, 1962 (1922).

Wright, Richard. *Native Son.* New York: New American Library, 1962.

Biographies

The biographical information furnished by these books can provide considerable insight into individual contributions to Afro-American culture. The data should not be used for student worksheets or for any activity that would replace actual contact with Afro-American music.

Anderson, Marian. *My Lord What a Morning.* New York: Franklin Watts, Inc., 1956.

Armstrong, Louis. *Satchmo: My Life in New Orleans.* Englewood Cliffs, New Jersey: Prentice-Hall, 1954.

Bailey, Pearl. *A Raw Pearl.* New York: Harcourt Brace Jovanovich, Inc., 1968.

Bradford, Perry. *Born With the Blues.* New York: Oak Publications, 1965.

Dance, Stanley. *The World of Duke Ellington.* New York: Charles Scribner and Sons, 1970.

Davis, Sammy, Jr. and J. Boyar. *Yes, I Can.* New York: Pocket Books, Inc., 1966.

Gammond, Peter. *Duke Ellington: His Life and Music.* London: Phoenix House, 1958.

Gitler, Ira (ed.). *Jazz Masters of the Forties.* New York: Macmillan, 1966.

Goldberg, Joe (ed.). *Jazz Masters of the Fifties.* New York: Macmillan, 1966.

Hadlock, Richard (ed.). *Jazz Masters of the Twenties.* New York: Macmillan, 1966.

Handy, W. C. *Father of the Blues.* New York: Macmillan, 1941.

Handy, W. C. *Negro Authors and Composers of the United States.* New York: Handy Brothers Music Company, 1938.

Hare, Maud Cuney. *Negro Musicians and Their Music.* Washington, D.C.: The Associated Publishers, 1936.

Heilbut, Tony. *The Gospel Sound.* New York: Simon and Schuster, 1971.
  A study of gospel singers including Bessie Griffin, James Cleveland, Sally Martin and Willie Mae Ford Smith. Includes a discography of gospel music.

Holiday, Billie and William Dufty. *Lady Day Sings the Blues.* New York: Doubleday, 1956.

Horricks, Raymond. *Count Basie and His Orchestra.* London: Victor Gollancs, 1957.

Hoyt, Edwin Palmer. *Paul Robeson: The American Othello.* New York: World Publishing Co., 1967.

Hughes, Langston. *Famous American Music Makers.* New York: Dodd, Mead & Company, 1955.

Hughes, Langston. *Famous Negro Music Makers.* New York: Dodd, Mead & Company, 1955.

Jackson, Mahalia, and E. M. Wylie. *Movin' on Up: The Mahalia Jackson Story.* New York: Hawthorn (Distributed by Arco Publishing Co., N.Y.), 1966.

Kirkeby, W. T. (in collaboration with Duncan Schiedt & Sinclair Traill). *Ain't Misbehavin': The Story of Fats Waller.* Mayfair, London: Peter Davies, Ltd., 1966.

Lambert, George E. *Duke Ellington.* New York: A. S. Barnes & Co., Inc., 1961.

Lomax, Alan. *Mr. Jelly Roll.* New York: Duell, Sloan and Pearce, 1950.

Moore, Carman. *Somebody's Angel Child: The Story of Bessie Smith*. New York: Thomas Y. Crowell Co., 1969.

Ramsey, Frederic and Charles E. Smith (eds.). *Been Here and Gone*. New Brunswick, New Jersey: Rutgers University Press, 1960.

Rollins, Charlemae. *Famous Entertainers of Stage, Screen and T.V.* New York: Dodd, Mead & Company, 1967.

Rollins, Charlemae. *They Showed the Way*. New York: Thomas Y. Crowell Co., 1964.

Sayers, W. C. Berwick. *Samuel Coleridge-Taylor, Musician: His Life and Letters*. London: Cassell & Co., Ltd., 1915.

Shapiro, Nat (ed.). *Jazz Makers*. New York: Holt, Rinehart & Winston, Inc., 1957.

Shaw, Arnold. *Belafonte*. Philadelphia: Chilton Book Co., 1960.

Smith, Willie-the-Lion. *Music on My Mind*. New York: Doubleday & Co., Inc., 1964.

Spellman, A. B. *Black Music; Four Lives*. New York: Schocken Books, 1970. A current edition of *Four Lives in the Bebop Business*.

Terkel, Studs. *Giants of Jazz*. New York: Thomas Y. Crowell Co., 1957.

Waters, Ethel and Charles Samuels. *His Eye Is on the Sparrow*. New York: Doubleday, 1951.

Wells, Dicky and Stanley Dance. *The Night People*. Boston: Crescendo Publishing Company, 1971.

William, Martin T. *Jazz Masters of New Orleans*. New York: Macmillan, 1967.

Books on Music

Allen, William F., Charles P. Ware and L. M. Garrison (eds.). *Slave Songs of the United States*. New York: Oak Publications, 1965 (Reprint from A. Simpson & Co., 1867).

   Includes an original collection of 136 songs compiled in 1867 by the authors. New piano arrangements and guitar chords are by Irving Schlein.

Baker, David. *Jazz Improvisation—A Comprehensive Method of Study for All Players*. Chicago: Maher Publications, 1969.

   For the school teacher, student, amateur and professional musician. Various aspects of jazz improvisation are treated. Content ranges from nomenclature through fundamental exercises in improvisation techniques to advanced concepts of jazz playing. Bibliographies and discographies are included.

Blesh, Rudi. *Shining Trumpets: A History of Jazz.* 2nd Edition. New York: A. Knopf, 1958.

Blesh, Rudi and Harriet Janis. *They All Played Ragtime.* 4th edition. New York: Oak Publications, 1971.

Butcher, Margaret Just and Alain Locke. *The Negro in American Culture.* New York: Alfred A. Knopf, 1956.
  Based on materials left by Alain Locke, this book is a survey dealing with the impact of blacks on American arts and literature.

Carawan, Guy (comp.). *We Shall Overcome! Songs of the Southern Freedom Movement.* New York: Oak Publications, 1963.

Carawan, Guy and Candie Carawan. *Ain't You Got a Right to the Tree of Life?* New York: Simon & Schuster, 1967.
  Contains songs of the people of Johns Island, South Carolina. The music was transcribed by Ethel Raim and recorded by the authors. A preface by Alan Lomax and a bibliography are included.

Chambers, Herbert Arthur (ed.). *The Treasury of Negro Spirituals.* New York: Emerson Books, 1963.

Charters, Samuel B. *The Bluesmen: The Story and the Music of the Men Who Made the Blues.* New York: Oak Publications, 1967.
  Includes information pertaining to singers from Mississippi, Alabama, and Texas covering a period up to the Second World War. Some consideration is given to relationships that exist between blues and African songs.

Charters, Samuel. *The Country Blues.* New York: Rinehart & Co., Inc., 1959.

Charters, Samuel. *The Poetry of the Blues.* New York: Oak Publications, 1963.

Charters, Samuel and Leonard Kunstadt. *Jazz: A History of the New York Scene.* Garden City, New York: Doubleday, 1962.

Coleridge-Taylor, Samuel. *Twenty-Four Negro Melodies.* Transcribed for the piano, with preface by Booker T. Washington. Boston: Oliver Ditson, 1905.

Courlander, Harold. *The Drum and the Hoe.* Berkeley and Los Angeles: University of California, 1960.

Describes the uses of instruments in the music of Haiti. Chapter 18 contains a description of the musical instruments of Haiti with sketches of drum design and construction.

Courlander, Harold. *Haiti Singing.* Chapel Hill: University of North Carolina Press, 1939.
Includes music and plates. Words of the songs are in Creole and English.

Courlander, Harold. *Negro Folk Music, U.S.A.* New York: Columbia University Press, 1963.

Courlander, Harold (collector). *Negro Songs from Alabama.* New York: Oak Publications, 1962.

De Lerma, Dominique-René, *et al. Black Music in Our Culture.* Kent, Ohio: Kent State University Press, 1970.
Subjects discussed by a wide range of music professionals are black music in the church, jazz history, black composers, avant-garde Negro dance and its influence on black music, and William Grant Still's viewpoint on black music. Also included are sample materials for teaching black music, faculty and student viewpoints, problems relative to publishing and recording music, and administrative problems of implementation, funding and staffing. Appendices include selected lists of recordings, film bibliography and sample syllabi.

De Lerma, Dominique-René (ed.). *Explorations in Black Music: The Seminar Program.* Bloomington, Indiana: The Black Music Center, 1971.

Dennison, Tim. *The Negro and His Amazing Music.* New York: Vintage Press, 1963.

Delaunay, Charles and George Avakian (eds.). *New Hot Discography: the Standard Directory of Recorded Jazz.* New York: Criterion, 1948.

Detroit Public Schools Workshop. *Afro-America Sings.* Detroit: Board of Education of the School District of the City of Detroit, 1971.
A songbook and guide containing Afro-American folk songs, contemporary selections and piano pieces. Includes teacher's guide.

Fernett, Gene. *Swing Out: Great Negro Dance Bands.* Midland, Michigan: Pendell Publishing Co., 1970.
Includes numerous photographs of jazz artists.

Fisher, Miles M. *Negro Slave Songs in the U.S.* New York: Citadel Press, 1963, or New York: Russell & Russell, 1968.

Garland, Phyl. *The Sound of Soul.* Chicago: Henry Regnery, 1969.
    A discussion of contemporary black music, which can be very useful for teachers.

Gentry, Linnell. *History and Encyclopedia of Country, Western and Gospel Music.* Nashville: Clairmont Corporation, 1969.

Greenway, John. *American Folksongs of Protest.* New York: Barnes, 1960.

Handy, W. C. *A Treasury of the Blues.* New York: A. and C. Boni, 1926.

Handy, W. C. *Blues, An Anthology.* New York: A. and C. Boni, 1926.

Hayward, Charles (ed.). *Folk Songs of the World.* New York: Bantam Books, 1968.

Hentoff, Nat and Albert J. McCarthy (eds.). *Jazz.* New York: Rinehart & Co., Inc., 1959.

Hentoff, Nat and Albert J. McCarthy. *Jazz, A People's Music.* New York: Citadel, 1948.

Hitchcock, H. Wiley. *Music in the United States: A Historical Introduction.* Englewood Cliffs, New Jersey: Prentice-Hall, 1969.

Hodier, Andre. *Jazz: Its Evolution and Essence* (translated by David Noakes). New York: Grove Press, Inc., 1956.

Howard, Joseph A. *Drums in the Americas.* New York: Oak Publications, 1967.

Jackson, George Pullen. *White and Negro Spirituals, Their Life Span and Kinship.* New York: J. J. Augustan, 1944.

Johnson, James Weldon and J. Rosamond Johnson. *The Book of American Negro Spirituals.* New York: The Viking Press, 1925 (Reprinted, 1969).

Jones, LeRoi. *Black Music.* New York: William Morrow & Co., 1967.
    A description of recent events and people in the world of jazz, with a brief discography and a few photographs.

Jones, LeRoi. *Blues People.* New York: William Morrow & Co., 1963.
    An historical overview of Afro-American music with an extremely important description of the effect of black and white attitudes on black music.

Keepnews, Orin and Bill Grauer. *A Pictorial History of Jazz.* New York: Crown Publishers, 1955 (Revised edition, 1966).

Keil, Charles. *Urban Blues*. Chicago: University of Chicago Press, 1966.

    A description of urban blues and the outstanding musicians identified with this style, with appendices and a few photographs.

Kofsky, Frank. *Black Nationalism and the Revolution in Music*. New York: Pathfinder Press, Inc., 1970.

Lawrence, Vera Brodsky (ed.). *The Collected Works of Scott Joplin*. 2 volumes. New York City: The New York Public Library, 1971.

    Volume 1, "Works for Piano," contains forty-four original selections (rags, marches, waltzes, and a tango), seven works written in collaboration with other composers, *The School of Ragtime* (six exercises for piano), and a posthumous work attributed to Joplin which was recently found on a piano roll played by him.

    Volume 2, "Works for Voice," contains the entire piano-vocal score of the opera, *Treemonisha,* three subsequently published and revised excerpts from *Treemonisha,* and nine songs. Introductory material is by Carman Moore.

Lawrence, Vera Brodsky (ed.). *The Piano Works of Louis Moreau Gottschalk*. New York: Arno Press and New York Times, 1969.

    A five-volume collection. Gottschalk's highly successful, virtuosic, Creole compositions are said to be derived from the composer's recollections of his life in New Orleans where he was deeply influenced by the songs, dances, jazz-like phrases and rhythms of the black people.

Lawrenz, Marguerite. *Bibliography and Index of Negro Music*. Detroit: Detroit Public Schools, Department of Music Education, 1968.

Leadbitter, Mike. *Delta Country Blues*. Bexhill-on-Sea: Blues Unlimited, 1968.

Leonard, Neil. *Jazz and the White Americans*. Chicago: University of Chicago Press, 1962.

Locke, Alain L. *The Negro and His Music*. Port Washington, New York: Kennikat Press, 1968. Kennikat Press series in Negro culture and history. (Reprint of an edition first published in 1936).

    This source is valuable for the reading references included at the end of some of the chapters.

Lomax, John A. *American Ballads and Folk Songs*. New York: Macmillan, 1934.

Lomax, John A. and Alan Lomax. *Folksong, U.S.A.* New York: Duell, Sloan, Pearce, 1947.

Lomax, John A. and Alan Lomax. *Our Singing Country*. New York: Macmillan, 1941.

McCarthy, Albert, *et al. Jazz on Record: A Critical Guide to the First Fifty Years (1917-1967)*. London: Hanover Books, Ltd., 1968.

Morath, Max (comp.). *One Hundred Ragtime Classics*. Denver: Donn Publishing Company, 1963.

Nettl, Bruno. *An Introduction to Folk Music in the United States*. Detroit: Wayne University Press, Wayne State University Studies, No. 7, 1960.

Nettl, Bruno. *Folk and Traditional Music of the Western Continents*. Englewood Cliffs, New Jersey: Prentice-Hall, Inc., 1965.
> Chapter 7, "African Music South of the Sahara," and Chapter 9, "Negro Folk Music in the New World," are of particular interest to students of black music.

Odum, Howard W. and Guy B. Johnson. *Negro Workaday Songs*. New York: Negro Universities Press, 1969 (Reprint from University of North Carolina Press, 1926).

Odum, Howard W. and Guy B. Johnson. *The Negro and His Songs*. Hatboro, Pennsylvania: Folklore Associates, 1925 (Reprint. New York: Negro Universities Press, 1968).

Oliver, Paul. *Aspects of the Blues Tradition*. New York: Oak Publications, 1970.

Oliver, Paul. *Blues Fell This Morning*. New York: Horizon Press, 1960.

Oliver, Paul. *Conversation with the Blues*. New York: Horizon Press, 1965.

Oliver, Paul. *The Meaning of the Blues*. New York: Collier Books, 1963.

Oliver, Paul. *Savannah Syncopators*. New York: Stein and Day, 1970.
> Discusses African retentions in the blues. Many slaves may have come from the savannah regions of Africa bringing to America music similar to that of the Griots. Brief notes, a record list, glossary and an index of tribes and people of the savannah are included.

Oliver, Paul. *The Story of the Blues*. Philadelphia: Chilton Book Co., 1969.
> The development of the blues is traced from field hollers to contemporary urban blues. A bibliography, discography and index are included.

Ostransky, Leroy. *The Anatomy of Jazz*. Seattle: University of Washington Press, 1960.

Patterson, Lindsay (ed.). *The Negro in Music and Art*. International Library of Negro Life and History, produced by The Association for the Study of Negro Life and History. Washington, D.C.: United Publishing Corporation, 1967.

    Includes numerous photographs of black artists. Highly recommended for classroom teachers.

Pleasants, Henry. *Serious Music and All That Jazz*. New York: Simon & Schuster, 1969.

    Pleasants' thesis is that concert music is being supplanted by the more relevant, expressive and imaginative sounds of the Afro-American idioms of jazz, blues, rock, pop and soul. He suggests that "we are now in the midst of what future musical historians may well designate as the Afro-American epoch." This book is a consideration of the music of this epoch, emphasizing its importance in the broad context of music history.

Poling, James. *Esquire's World of Jazz*. New York: Esquire, Inc., 1962. Distributed by Grosset & Dunlap, Publishers.

    Includes numerous pictures, discussions of style, and annotated discography. An excellent source for teachers.

Roxon, Lillian. *Rock Encyclopedia*. New York: Workman Publishing Co., 1969.

    Presents information on performers, styles and recordings.

Schuller, Gunther. *Early Jazz: Its Roots and Musical Development*. New York: Oxford University Press, 1968.

    The first of a projected two-volume survey, this book examines the origins of jazz and analyzes its development during the twenties.

Shapiro, Nat and Nat Hentoff. *Hear Me Talkin' to Ya*. New York: Dover Publications, Inc., 1955.

Shaw, Arnold. *The World of Soul: Black American's Contribution to the Pop Music Scene*. New York: Cowles Book Co., 1970.

Silverman, Jerry. *Folk Blues*. New York: Oak Publications, 1968.

Southern, Eileen. *The Music of Black Americans: A History*. New York: W. W. Norton & Co., Inc., 1971.

    Concerns itself with two aspects of black musical influence in America: (1) that the black musician has created new musical traditions, and (2) that since his arrival in the New World he has contributed to and enriched the European-based musical traditions. Contains a comprehensive compilation of black American musicians.

Stearns, Marshall. *Jazz Dance: The American Vernacular Dance*. New York: Macmillan Press, 1968.

Stearns, Marshall. *The Story of Jazz*. New York: Mentor Books, 1958.
A comprehensive study of jazz, chronologically arranged, with an extensive bibliography, discography and syllabus of lectures. Also included are pictures and a chart showing the development of Afro-American music.

Tally, Thomas W. (comp.). *Negro Folk Rhythms, Wise and Otherwise*. Port Washington, New York: Kennikat Press, 1968. Kennikat Press series in Negro culture and history.

Tanner, Paul O. and Maria Gerow. *A Study of Jazz*. Revised edition. Dubuque, Iowa: William C. Brown Company, Publishers, 1964.

Thurman, Howard. *Deep River: Reflections on the Religious Insight of Certain of the Negro Spirituals*. New York: Harper, 1955.

Thurman, Howard. *The Negro Spiritual Speaks of Life and Death*. New York: Harper, 1947. The Ingersoll Lecture, Harvard University, 1947.

Trotter, James M. *Music and Some Highly Musical People*. Boston: Lee & Shepard, 1878 (Reprint. Chicago: Afro-Am Press, 1969).
An early source offering an interesting historical perspective. Chapters dealing with music are followed by résumés of the lives of black musicians, their portraits and an appendix containing musical scores by black composers.

Ulanov, Barry. *Handbook of Jazz*. New York: Viking Press, 1960.

White, Newman Ivey. *American Negro Folk Songs*. Hatboro, Pennsylvania: Forklore Associates, 1965 (First edition, 1928).

Williams, Martin T. (ed.). *The Art of Jazz*. New York: Oxford University Press, 1959.

Williams, Martin T. (ed.). *Jazz Panorama*. New York: Collier Books, 1967.

Williams, Martin T. *The Jazz Tradition*. New York: Oxford University Press, 1970.

Williams, Martin T. *Where's the Melody?* New York: Pantheon Books, 1969.
Deals with such basic questions as how to listen to jazz, what jazz musicians do with a melody as they improvise, how jazz is composed, and where jazz came from. Includes suggestions for recommended listening and a brief outline of the development of jazz. Numerous perform-

ing and recording jazz personalities are discussed. The final section consists of Williams' personal comments as a listener and critic. The book ends with a discussion of developments in jazz during the 1960's.

Work, John W. *American Negro Songs*. Philadelphia: Theodore Presser Co., 1948.
    Discusses black American music such as the spiritual, the blues and work songs. Most of the text contains Mr. Work's arrangements of representative examples from these traditions. A bibliography and index are included.

Articles on Music

"A Musical Novelty," *American Musician* (June 24, 1911).

"A Symposium on Louis Armstrong: The Man Who Revolutionized Jazz," *The Saturday Review* (July 4, 1970).
    A cover story and three articles discuss the life, artistic development and influence of Louis Armstrong on jazz. Authors and titles of material include: I. Stanley Dance, "Louis Armstrong, An American Original"; II. Bud Freeman, "The Father and His Flock"; III. Milt Gabler, "My Thousand-Year Man"; IV. Jack Bradley, "Trumpet Fanfare—A Discussion of Louis Armstrong with Three Trumpet Players: Billy Butterfield, Ray Nance and Clark Terry."

Berger, Monroe. "Jazz: Resistance to a Diffusion of a Cultural Pattern," *Journal of Negro History*. Vol. 32 (October 1947), pp. 461-494.

"Black America, 1970," *Time Magazine* (April 6, 1970).
    This issue is devoted to the role of the black man in America today. Most sections deal with significant aspects of the life of the American black, including his progress— or lack of it—in American society. Some topics covered are: the press, music, art, theater, the law, modern living, sports, and politics. Following each topic, a situation report is given summarizing related current activities.

"Black Arts for Black Youth," *The Saturday Review* (July 18, 1970).
    Contains articles by Don D. Bushnell and Topper Carew. John B. Hightower, director of the Museum of Modern Art, summed up the articles in this issue by saying: "We are being taught by the ghettos that the arts are about people—the way they move, the things they see, the sounds they make. It may be that the ghettos will teach us once again

how to sing about ourselves in a way that reminds us that the beauty and quality of all our lives and the content of our arts are inseparable."

Bontemps, Arna. "Rock, Church, Rock," *Common Grounds*. Vol. 3 (Autumn 1942), pp. 75-80.

Campbell, S. Brunson. "Ragtime Begins," *The Record Changer* (March 1948), p. 8.

Campbell, S. Brunson and Roy Carew. "Sedalia, Missouri, Cradle of Ragtime," *The Record Changer* (May and June 1945).

Carew, Roy. "Treemonisha," *The Record Changer* (October 1946), p. 17.

Carew, Roy and Don Fowler. "Scott Joplin, Overlooked Genius," *The Record Changer* (September, October and December 1944).

Charters, Ann. "The First Negro Folk Opera: Treemonisha," *Jazz Monthly* (August 1962), p. 6.

Colvig, Richard. "Black Music," *Choice*—Book for College Libraries, Association of College and Research Libraries (November 1969), pp. 1169-1179.
    A brief, annotated bibliography of African and Afro-American music. It was compiled especially for public and smaller college libraries, and includes representative selections of English language monographs dealing with black contributions to music.

Cray, Ed. "An Acculturative Continuum for Negro Folk Song in the United States," *Ethnomusicology*. Vol. 5, No. 1 (1961), pp. 10-15.
    An examination of black folk music in terms of acculturation. Cray suggests that Negro music traditions represent a fusion of African and European musical traits, styles and techniques, and that black tradition parallels and/or complements the white one. He identifies three levels of appeal of Negro music: folk, popular and art, and he proposes that these levels exist as part of an acculturative continuum. The discussion is based on the idea that acculturation embraces those phenomena that result when groups of individuals from different cultures come into continuous firsthand contact. Subsequent changes then evolve in the culture patterns of one or both groups, *with* the added concept of force, either internal or external, triggering the changes. Certain forces triggering these changes in black folk music in the United States are discussed.

" 'Deep River' Popularizes a Composer: The Rise and Progress of Harry T. Burleigh Through His Negro Melodies into the Large Vogue of Song Recitals," *Boston Evening Transcript* (March 10, 1917).

Downey, James C. "Revivalism, The Gospel Songs and Social Reform," *Ethnomusicology*. Vol. 9, No. 2 (1965), pp. 115-125.

Duncan, John. "Negro Composers of Opera," *The Negro History Bulletin*. Vol. 29 (January 1966), pp. 79-80.

Farmer, James. "People Have to be What They Are," *Music Educators Journal*. Vol. 56 (May 1970), pp. 38-41.

Heckman, Don. "Five Decades of Rhythm and Blues," *The Many Worlds of Music*. Broadcast Music, Inc., New York (Summer 1969).
    A special issue devoted heavily to black music.

Herskovits, Melville Jean. "Drums and Drummers in Afro-Brazilian Cult Life," *Music Quarterly*. Vol. 30, No. 4 (1944), pp. 447-492.

Herskovits, Melville Jean. "Negro Art: African and American," *Journal of Social Forces*. Vol. 5 (1926), pp. 291-298.

Herzog, George. "African Influence on North American Indian Music," *Christian Science Monitor* (September 15, 1939).

Hitchcock, H. Wiley. "Ragtime of the Higher Class," *Stereo Review* (April 1971).

Johnson, Earle H. "The Need for Research in History of American Music," *The Journal of Research in Music Education*. Vol. 6, No. 1 (Spring 1966), pp. 73-84.

Jones, A. M. "Blue Notes and Hot Rhythm," *African Music*. Vol. 1 (June 1951), pp. 9-12.

Laubenstein, Paul Fritz. "Race Values in Afro-American Music," *Musical Quarterly*. Vol. 16 (July 1930), pp. 378-430.

Lovell, John, Jr. "Social Implications of Negro Spirituals," *Journal of Negro Education*. Vol. 8 (1939), pp. 642-643.

McCorkle, Donald M. "Finding a Place for American Studies in American Musicology," *Journal of the American Musicological Society*. Vol. 19 (Spring 1958), pp. 73-84.

McKay, George Frederick. "Toward a Cultural Definition," *The Journal of Research in Music Education*. Vol. 3 (Fall 1955), pp. 92-100.

McKinney, Harold. "Negro Music: A Definitive American Expression," *Negro History Bulletin*. Vol. 27 (February 1964).

Merriam, Alan P. "Jazz—The Word," *Ethnomusicology*. Vol. 12 (September 1968), pp. 373-396.

Merriam, Alan P. "Music in American Culture," *American Anthropologist*. Vol. 57 (1955), pp. 1173-1181.
> Discussion of four major musical streams in American culture: academic music, folk music of the white communities, jazz and popular music (as differentiated from jazz). Merriam's discussion of jazz rests on the premise that black musical expression is derived from both European and African influences, the result being the emergence of a music that is different from either.

Meyer, Leonard B. "Universalism and Relativism in the Study of Ethnic Music," *Ethnomusicology*. Vol. 4, No. 2 (1960), pp. 49-54.
> An article attacking the strong tendency toward simplistic monism that has marked our thinking in the area of ethnic music. The author points out that the idea of music as a universal language has long been discredited and that the equally monistic relativism which sought to study each culture and each music "in its own terms" has also failed to produce new insights into the nature of man, culture and their interrelationships. Meyer suggests that many of the observed failures occurred because they avoided cross-cultural questions. He emphasizes that parsimony governs our perception of music through the unconscious operation of principles such as those of simplicity and good shape. Further, he points out that such a principle also influences explanations of the nature of music, the development of musical styles, and the relations of music to the culture in which it arises. A particular value of this article is that it puts into perspective the use of such common terms as melody, mode, rhythm and form.

Music Educators Journal. Vol. 56 (January 1970).
> A special report dealing with issues in urban music education that includes several valuable articles relating to music and the black child. Some areas discussed are: urban culture, school administrators, successful teaching, course content and teacher education.

Nettl, Bruno. "Change in Folk and Primitive Music: A Survey of Methods and Studies," *Journal of the American Musicological Society*. Vol. 8 (Summer 1955), pp. 101-109.

Schonberg, Harold C. "Scholars, Get Busy on Scott Joplin!" *New York Times* (January 24, 1971).

Sigurd, Jacques. "Portrait of the Artist as a Young Dancer," *The Saturday Review* (September 14, 1968), p. 57.

A brief survey of the life and artistic development of the gifted black artist, painter, dancer and actor: Geoffrey Holder.

Slotkin, J. S. "Jazz and Its Forerunners as an Example of Acculturation," *American Sociological Review.* Vol. 8 (1943), pp. 570-575.

Standifer, James A. "Choosing An Approach to Black Studies in Music," *The School Musician Director and Teacher.* Vol. 41 (December 1969), p. 60.

A discussion of ways in which black music should be used in the school curriculum. Various means are presented of putting questions of black music into perspective for individuals struggling with this question in emerging black studies programs.

Still, William Grant. "Fifty Years of Progress in Music," *The Pittsburgh Courier* (November 11, 1950), p. 15.

Still, William Grant. "Music, A Vital Factor in America's Racial Problems," *The Australian Musical News* (November 1, 1948).

Tallmadge, William H. "Dr. Watts and Mahalia Jackson," *Ethnomusicology.* Vol. 5 (May 1961), pp. 95-99.

A discussion of a church singing style known as "lining-out" (sometimes called "long-meter" or "Dr. Watts"). The author points out that the style still exists among elderly blacks in America. Specific recordings are listed that provide examples of "lining-out." The author uses the following example in discussing a type of "lining-out" as practiced in black churches and sometimes known as "surge singing."

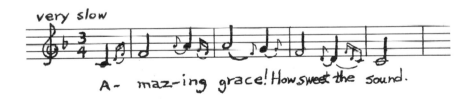

This example illustrates a style of contemporary gospel singing derived from "lining-out":

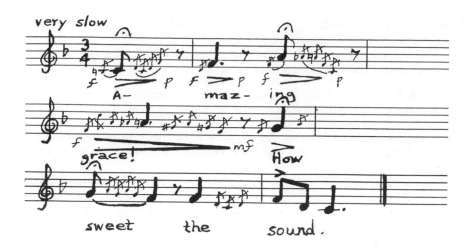

Tallmadge, William H. "The Responsorial and Antiphonal Practices in Gospel Song," *Ethnomusicology.* Vol. 12 (May 1968), pp. 219-238.

Taylor, Clifford. "The Design of Culture—and the Afro-Asian Revolution," *Encounter* (November 1968), pp. 41-47.

Terry, Walter. "The Conga, The Pachanga, and the Cha-Cha-Cha," *The Saturday Review* (September 14, 1968), p. 59.

Thieme, Darius. "Negro Folk Song Scholarship in the United States," *African Music.* Vol. 2, No. 3 (1960), pp. 67-72.

Thompson, Kay C. "Lottie Joplin," *The Record Changer* (October 1950), p. 8.

Waterman, Guy. "A Survey of Ragtime," *The Record Changer* (1955), p. 7 (Also found in: Williams, *The Art of Jazz,* see page 60).

Waterman, Guy. "Joplin's Late Rags, An Analysis," *The Record Changer* (1955), p. 5.

Waterman, Richard Alan. "African Influence on American Negro Music," in *Acculturation in the Americas,* edited by Sol Tax. Chicago: University of Chicago Press, 1952, pp. 209-218 (Reprint, New York, 1967).
    A discussion of some of the African characteristics that are found in Afro-American music.

Waterman, Richard Alan. "Gospel Hymns of a Negro Church in Chicago," *International Folk Music Journal.* Vol. 3 (1951), pp. 87-93.

Waterman, Richard Alan. "Hot Rhythm in Negro Music," *Journal of the American Musicological Society.* Vol. 1 (1948), pp. 24-37.

    Waterman traces "hot" rhythm through African, American folk and jazz styles. There are transcriptions of jazz materials and of songs from the West Indies.

Waterman, Richard Alan. "On Flogging a Dead Horse: Lessons Learned from the Africanism Controversy," *Ethnomusicology.* Vol. 7 (May 1963), pp. 83-87.

Williams, Martin. "The Bystander," *Down Beat* (June 20, 1963).

Williams-Jones, Pearl. "Afro-American Gospel Music," *Final Report,* Project in African Music, Howard University (1970), pp. 199-219.

Yancy, Henrietta Miller. "The Contribution of the American Negro to the Music Culture of the Country," *The School Musician Director and Teacher.* Vol. 41 (March 1970).

Books on Poetry

Adoff, Arnold (ed.). *Black Out Loud: An Anthology of Modern Poems by Black Americans.* New York: Macmillan, 1970.

    A fine collection of poems on such subjects as being black, the black poet and slain leaders. Includes illustrations.

Adoff, Arnold (ed.). *I am the Darker Brother; an Anthology of Modern Poems by Negro Americans.* New York: Macmillan Co., 1968.

Bontemps, Arna. *American Negro Poetry.* New York: Hill and Wang, 1963.

Breman, Paul (ed.). *Sixes and Sevens; an Anthology of New Poetry.* London: P. Breman, 1962.

    Includes works by six poets with their statements concerning whether being black colors one's writings.

Hayden, Robert E. *Kaleidoscope.* New York: Harcourt Brace Jovanovich, Inc., 1967.

    Approaches poetic content purely as an art form.

Hughes, Langston. *Ask Your Mama: 12 Moods for Jazz.* New York: Alfred A. Knopf, 1969.

    Langston Hughes presents a sequence of jazz poetry. Each poem is accompanied with directions for the inclusion of appropriate music, including instrumentation and method of production. The traditional folk melody of the "Hesitation Blues" is the leitmotif for the poems. Other recognizable melodies are employed and room is given for spontaneous jazz improvisation, particularly between verses where the voice pauses.

Hughes, Langston (ed.). *Poems from Black Africa*. Bloomington: Indiana University Press, 1969.

Hughes, Langston and Arna Bontemps (eds.). *The Poetry of the Negro—1746-1949*. Garden City, New York: Doubleday & Company, Inc., 1949.

Kgositsile, Keorapetse. *My Name is Afrika*. Garden City, New York: Doubleday & Company, Inc., 1971.
This collection presents a poetic definition of the African and American black experience. The poet laments the dilemmas prevalent in Africa and the ghettos of black America.

Lomax, Alan and Abdul Raoul (eds.). *Three Thousand Years of Black Poetry: An Anthology*. New York: Dodd, Mead & Co., 1970.

Moore, Gerald and Ulli Beier (eds.). *Modern Poetry from Africa*. London: Penguin Books, 1966.

Randall, Dudley (ed.). *The Black Poets: An Anthology*. New York: Bantam Books, 1971.

Books for Elementary Grades

The following entries might be helpful as supportive material for the study of Afro-American music. This abridged list merely suggests the increasing availability of books on black Americans written for younger students.

Non-fiction

Bontemps, Arna Wendell (comp.). *Golden Slippers, an Anthology of Negro Poetry for Young Readers*. New York: Harper and Brothers, 1941.

Cohen, Robert. *Color of Man*. New York: Random House, 1968.

Hughes, Langston. *First Book of Jazz*. New York: Franklin Watts, Inc., 1955.

Hughes, Langston and Milton Meltzer. *Pictorial History of the Negro in America*. 3rd revised edition. New York: Crown Publishers, Inc., 1968.

Jackson, M. M. (ed.). *Bibliography of Negro History and Culture for Young Readers*. Pittsburgh: Published for Atlanta University by the University of Pittsburgh Press, 1969.

Meltzer, Milton (ed.). *In Their Own Words, A History of the American Negro.* Volumes 1, 2 and 3. 1916-1966. New York: Crown Publishers, Inc., 1967.

Fiction and Folklore

Armstrong, William. *Sounder.* New York: Harper & Row Publishers, Inc., 1967.

Baker, Betty. *Walk the World's Rim.* New York: Harper & Row Publishers, Inc., 1965.

Boston, Lucy Maria. *Treasure of Green Knowe.* New York: Harcourt Brace Jovanovich, Inc., 1958.

Carlson, Natalie Savage. *The Empty Schoolhouse.* New York: Harper & Row Publishers, Inc., 1965.

Caudill, Rebecca. *A Certain Small Shepherd.* New York: Holt, Rinehart & Winston, Inc., 1965.

Faulkner, Georgene and J. L. Becker. *Melindy's Medal.* New York: Julian Messner, Inc., 1945.

Fritz, Jean. *Brady.* New York: Coward-McCann, Inc., 1960.

Gates, Doris. *Little Vic.* New York: Viking Press, Inc., 1951.

Grosvenor, Kali. *Poems by Kali.* Garden City, N.Y.: Doubleday, 1970.

Hamilton, Virginia. *Zeeley.* New York: Macmillan, 1967.

Keats, Ezra Jack. *John Henry: An American Legend.* New York: Pantheon Books, Inc., 1965.

Levy, Mimi Cooper. *Corrie and the Yankee.* New York: Viking Press, Inc., 1959.

Scott, Ann Herbert. *Sam.* New York: McGraw-Hill Co., 1968.

Shotwell, Louisa Rossiter. *Roosevelt Grady.* New York: World Publishing Co., 1963.

Steptoe, John. *Stevie.* New York: Harper and Row, 1969.

Stevenson, William. *The Bushbabies.* Boston: Houghton Mifflin Co., 1965.

Trevino, Elizabeth Borton de. *I, Juan de Pareja.* New York: Farrar, Straus and Giroux, Inc., 1965.

Tunis, John Roberts. *All-American.* New York: Harcourt Brace Jovanovich, Inc., 1942.

Biographies

Adoff, Arnold. *Malcolm* X. New York: Thomas Y. Crowell Co., 1970.

Douglass, Frederick. *Life and Times of Frederick Douglass*. Adapted by Barbara Ritchie. New York: Thomas Y. Crowell Co., 1966.

Graham, Shirley and G. D. Lipscomb. *Doctor George Washington Carver: Scientist*. New York: Julian Messner, Inc., 1944.

Johnston, Johanna. *Special Bravery*. New York: Dodd, Mead & Co., 1967.

McNeer, May Yonge and L. K. Ward. *Armed with Courage*. New York: Abingdon Press, 1957.

Petry, Ann. *Harriet Tubman: Conductor of the Underground Railroad*. New York: Thomas Y. Crowell Co., 1955.

Rowe, Jeanne A. *Album of Martin Luther King, Jr*. New York: Franklin Watts, Inc., 1970.

Sterling, Dorothy. *Freedom Train*. New York: Doubleday & Co., Inc., 1954.

Sterne, Emma Gelders. *Mary Macleod Bethune*. New York: Alfred A. Knopf, Inc., 1957.

Swift, Hildegard Hoyt. *Railroad to Freedom*. New York: Harcourt Brace Jovanovich, Inc., 1932.

Yates, Elizabeth. *Amos Fortune, Free Man*. New York: E. P. Dutton & Co., Inc., 1950.

ADDITIONAL MATERIALS

Periodicals Regularly Containing Articles on Afro-American Music

Afro-American. 628 North Eutaw Street, Baltimore, Maryland.

Afro-American Music Opportunities Association. AAMOA Reports. Box 662, Minneapolis, Minnesota 55440.

American Anthropologist. American Anthropological Association. 1530 P Street, N.W., Washington, D.C.

American Jazz Review. American Jazz Club, Flushing, New York.

American Musical Digest. 245 W. 52nd Street, New York, N.Y. 10019. (Subscription address: MIT Press, Cambridge, Massachusetts 02142).

Billboard. 165 West 46th Street, New York, N.Y. 10036.

Black Music Review. 50 Ann Street, West Pittston, Pennsylvania 18643.

Black Poetry Journal. 1308 Masonic Avenue, Apt. 4, San Francisco, California 94117.

Black Scholar. The Black World Foundation. P.O. Box 908, Sausalito, California 94965.

Blues Research. 65 Grand Avenue, Brooklyn, N.Y. 11205.

Blues Unlimited. 38A Sackville Road, Bexhill-on-Sea, Sussex, England.

Blues World. 22 Manor Crescent, Knutsford, Cheshire, England.

BMI The Many Worlds of Music. Broadcast Music, Inc., New York, N.Y.

Chicago Daily Defender. Chicago, Illinois.

Collectors Classics. 38A Sackville Road, Bexhill-on-Sea, Sussex, England.

Cricket. Box 663, Newark, New Jersey.

Crisis. NAACP, 1790 Broadway, New York, N.Y. 10019.

Down Beat. Maher Publications, 222 West Adams Street, Chicago, Illinois 60606.

Ebony. Johnson Publishing Co., 1820 South Michigan Avenue, Chicago, Illinois 60616.

Ethnomusicology. Society for Ethnomusicology, Middletown, Connecticut.

Gospel News Journal. Philadelphia, Pennsylvania.

Gospel Rama Magazine. Gospelrama Publishing Co., Washington, D.C.

Gospel Reporter. New York, N.Y.

International Folk Music Council Bulletin (or) *Journal.* Department of Music, Queens University, Kingston, Ontario.

Jazz: A Quarterly of American Music. Jazz Publications, Inc., 2835 Asby Avenue, Berkeley, California.

Jazz Information. New York, N.Y.

Jazz Journal. Jazz Journal Ltd., The Cottage, 27 Willow Vale, London W. 12, England.

Jazz and Pop. Jazz Press, New York.

Jazz Report Magazine. 357 Leighton Drive, Ventura, California.

Jazz Review. New York. Reprinted by Kraus, New York, N.Y.

Jazz Times. British Jazz Society, 10 Southfield Gardens, Twickenham, Middlesex, England.

Jet. Johnson Publishing Co., 1820 South Michigan Avenue, Chicago, Illinois 60616.

Journal of American Folklore. American Folklore Society, University of Texas Press, Box 7819, Austin, Texas 78712.

Journal of Black Poetry. 922 Haight Street, San Francisco, California.

Journal of Negro History. Association for the Study of Negro Life and History, Inc., 1538 9th Street, N.W., Washington, D.C.

Michigan Chronicle. 479 Leadyard, Detroit, Michigan.

Negro Music Journal. 2 volumes, 1902-1903 (Reprint). Reproduction of the contents of the original publication, including articles, advertisements and photographs. Westport, Connecticut: Negro Universities Press, 1970.

Negro Press Digest. New York Chapter of the American Jewish Committee, 165 East 56th Street, New York, N.Y. 10022.

New York Amsterdam News. Powell-Savory Corporation, 2340 Eighth Avenue, New York, N.Y. 10027.

Pittsburgh Courier. 2628 Centre Avenue, Pittsburgh, Pennsylvania 15219.

Soul. Adelaide Street, Box 1047, Toronto 1, Ontario.

Soul Time. Black American, Inc., 200 West 149th Street, New York, N.Y. 10039.

Sounds and Fury. Taylor-Franklin Publishers, New York, N.Y.

The Southern Workman. Hampton Institute, Hampton, Virginia.

Urban West. 593 Market Street, San Francisco, California 94105.

Research

Completed Dissertations

Allison, Roland Lewis. "Classification of the Vocal Works of Harry T. Burleigh (1866-1949) and Some Suggestions for Their Use in Teaching Diction in Singing." Ph.D., Indiana University, 1966.

Baskerville, David Ross. "Jazz Influence on Art Music to Mid-Century." Ph.D., University of California, Los Angeles, 1965.

Belton, Geneva R. "The Contributions of Negro Music and Musicians in World War II." M.M., Northwestern University, 1946.

Braithwaite, Coleridge. "A Survey of the Lives and Creative Activities of Some Negro Composers." Ed.D., Columbia University, Teachers College, 1952.

Collins, Leslie Morgan. "A Song, A Dance and A Play: An Interpretative Study of Three American Artists (M. Anderson, P. Robeson, and K. Dunham)." Ph.D., Case Western Reserve University, 1945.

Daughtry, Willa E. "Sissieretta Jones: A Study of the Negro's Contribution to Nineteenth Century American Concert and Theatrical Life." Ph.D., Syracuse University, 1968.

Elder, Jacob Delworth. "Evolution of the Traditional Calypso of Trinidad and Tobago, A Socio-Historical Analysis of Song-Change." Ph.D., University of Pennsylvania, 1966.

Foreman, Ronald Clifford, Jr. "Jazz and Race Records, 1920-1932: Their Origins and Their Significance for the Record Industry and Society." Ph.D., University of Illinois, 1968.

George, Zelma Watson. "A Guide to Negro Music: An Annotated Bibliography of Negro Music and Art Music by Negro Composers." Ed.D., New York University, 1953.

Gold, Robert S. "A Jazz Lexicon." Ph.D., New York University, 1962.

Hansen, Chadwick Clark, "The Age of Jazz, A Study of Jazz in its Cultural Context." Ph.D., The University of Minnesota, 1956.

Jones, Bessie. "A Descriptive and Analytical Study of the American Negro Folklore." George Peabody College, 1968.

Keys, Charles F. "The Development and Significance of a Collection of Negro Folk Songs for Use in Junior High Schools." University of Cincinnati, Teachers College, 1943.

Lekis, Lisa. "The Origin and Development of Ethnic Caribbean Dance and Music." Ph.D., The University of Florida, 1956.

McBrier, Vivian Flagg. "The Life and Works of Robert Nathaniel Dett." Ph.D., Catholic University, 1967.

McCoy, James A. "The Bomba and Aguinaldo of Puerto Rico As They Have Evolved From Indigenous, African and European Cultures." Ph.D., Florida State University, 1968.

McLeod, Norma. "Some Techniques of Analysis for Non-Western Music." Ph.D., Northwestern University, 1966.

Merrit, Nancy G. "Negro Spirituals in American Collections: A Handbook for Students Studying Negro Spirituals." M.A., Howard University, 1940.

Miller, Kurt Robert. "Heroes Found in Song Texts From Folk Music of the United States (Volumes I and II)." D.M.A., University of Southern California, 1963.

Moore, Robert Steele. "Blues People—Original Composition Based on Texts from LeRoi Jones, Bob Kaufman, and Kenneth Patchen." Ph.D., State University of Iowa, 1969.

Parker, John W. "American Popular Music: An Emerging Field of Academic Study." Ed.D., University of Kentucky, 1962.

Patterson, Cecil Lloyd. "A Different Drum, The Image of the Negro in the Nineteenth Century Popular Song Books." Ph.D., The University of Pennsylvania, 1961.

Patterson, Perry Willis. "A Critical Study of the Jazz-Vaudeville Drama (1923-1934) in the United States." Ph.D., University of Denver, 1965.

Pyke, Launcelot, II. "Jazz, 1920-1927: An Analytical Study." 2 volumes. Ph.D., State University of Iowa, 1962.

Ricks, George Robinson. "Some Aspects of the Religious Music of the United States Negro: An Ethnomusicological Study with Special Emphasis on the Gospel Tradition." Ph.D. (Anthropology), Northwestern University, 1960.

Shockett, Bernard I. "A Stylistic Study of the Blues as Recorded by Jazz Instrumentalists, 1917-1931." Ph.D., New York University, 1964.

Simpson, Ralph Ricardo. "William Grant Still, The Man and His Music." Ph.D., Michigan State University, 1964.

Smith, Hugh L., Jr. "The Literary Manifestation of a Liberal Romanticism in American Jazz." Ph.D., University of New Mexico, 1955.

Southern, Eileen Stanza (Jackson). "The Use of Negro Folksong in Symphonic Form." M.A., University of Chicago, 1941.

Stebbins, Robert Alan. "The Jazz Community: The Sociology of a Musical Sub-Culture." Ph.D. (Sociology), University of Minnesota, 1964.

Thompson, Leon Everett. "A Historical and Stylistic Analysis of the Music of William Grant Still and Thematic Catalogue of His Work." D.M.A., University of Southern California, 1967.

Waterman, Richard A. "African Patterns in Trinidad Negro Music." Ph.D. (Anthropology), Northwestern University, 1943. (Includes materials from M. Kolinski's *Die Musick Westafrikas.*)

Approved Dissertations in Progress

The following entries are approved doctoral dissertations in progress as of January 1, 1971. Source: *Council for Research in Music Education.* Champaign, Illinois: University of Illinois.

Appleton, Clyde R. "The Comparative Preferential Response of Black and White College Students to Black and White Folk and Popular Musical Styles." New York University.

Books, Tilford. "A Historical Study of the Negro Composer and His Role in American Society: A Source Book for Teachers." Washington University.

Carter, Warrick. "Ethnic Music as a Source for the Musical Development and Enrichment of Culturally Different Students in General Music Classes." Michigan State University.

Cole, William S. "The Culturally Disadvantaged Teachers or How Will Urban Black Children Ever Learn About Their Music in the American Public School System." Wesleyan University (Connecticut).

Ferriano, Frank, Jr. "Stage Bands/Jazz Ensembles in Music Education: 1945-1970." Columbia University.

Hores, Robert G. "A Comparative Study of Visual and Aural Orientation Approaches to Jazz Improvisation With Implications for Instruction." Indiana University.

McCarroll, Jesse. "Black Influence on Southern White Protestant Church Music During Slavery." Columbia University.

McCauley, John. "Jazz Improvisation for the B-Flat Soprano Trumpet: A Text for Teaching Basic Theoretical Performance Principles." Louisiana State University.

Schmid, William R. "Introduction to Primitive, Oriental and Folk Music: The

Synthesis of a New Course for the Undergraduate Music Curriculum." Eastman School of Music of the University of Rochester.

Sprague, Eugene. "Jazz Style in the Late Forties and Early Fifties." Columbia University.

Taylor, John A. "The Emergence of the Black Performing Musician in the American Symphony Orchestra." Indiana University.

Taylor, John. "The Sociological and Psychological Implications of the Texts of the Antibellum Negro Spirituals." University of Northern Colorado (Greeley).

Black Collections

Centers that house collections of black contributions to American culture are emerging throughout the United States. The following sources should prove helpful to individuals needing appropriate materials.

Archives of Traditional Music, Folklore Institute, Indiana University, Bloomington, Indiana.
> Collection of phonograph recordings (music and spoken) representing cultures from all parts of the world; includes many holdings of African and Afro-American music.

Black Music Center, Indiana University, Bloomington, Indiana.
> Serves as a clearing house and reference center for the documentation of black music history. Sponsors annual seminars and publishes materials.

Carl VanVechten Collection, Fisk University Library, Nashville, Tennessee.

Cleveland Hall Collection, Chicago Public Library, Chicago, Illinois.

E. Azalia Hackley Collection, Detroit Public Library, Detroit, Michigan.

Historical Society of Pennsylvania, 1300 Locust Street, Philadelphia, Pennsylvania.

Library of Congress, Washington, D.C.

Moreland Collection, Howard University, Washington, D.C.

National Center of Afro-American Artists, Elma Lewis School of Fine Arts, Inc., Dorchester, Massachusetts.

Philadelphia Library Company, 1300 Locust Street, Philadelphia, Pennsylvania.

Schomburg Collection of Negro Literature and History, New York Public Library, New York City.

World Affairs Council, 1300 Market Street, Philadelphia, Pennsylvania.

Publishers of Reprints

The following companies currently are making available many out-of-print articles and books on the Afro-American and his contributions.

Afro-Am Books, Inc.
133 South Racine Avenue
Chicago, Illinois 60607

Afro-Am Publishing Company, Inc.
1727 South Indiana Avenue
Chicago, Illinois 60616

AMS Press, Inc. *(Black Studies Program Reprint: Literature of the Black Experience)*
56 East 13th Street
New York, N.Y. 10003

Arno Press, Inc. *(The American Negro: His History and Literature)*
330 Madison Avenue
New York, N.Y. 10017

Atheneum Publishers *(Studies in American Negro Life)*
122 East 42nd Street
New York, N.Y. 10017

Bell & Howell (Publishing the Afro-American collection at Atlanta University)
Cleveland-Mansfield Road
Wooster, Ohio 44691

Bobbs-Merrill Co. (Primarily Afro-American literature and history)
4300 West 62nd Street
Indianapolis, Indiana 46268

Collier-Macmillan Library Service (Afro-American literary works)
866 Third Avenue
New York, N.Y. 10022

G. K. Hall Company (Reproducing in book form from microfilm the complete

Schomburg collection of the New York Public Library. See page 77 and 3M listing below.)
70 Lincoln Street
Boston, Massachusetts 02111

Johnson Reprint Corporation *(The Basic Afro-American Reprint Library)*
111 Fifth Avenue
New York, N.Y. 10003

3M Corporation (Currently microfilming the complete Schomburg collection of the New York Public Library. See page 77)
3M Center
St. Paul, Minnesota 55101

Mnemosyne Publishing Company, Inc. (Reissuing material from Fisk University's Afro-American collections)
54 Southwest Seventh Street
Miami, Florida 33130

The Negro Universities Press *(The Black Experience in America)*
51 Riverside Avenue
Westport, Connecticut 06880

Tapes, Films and Film Strips

(see page 15 for list of film sources)

Adventures in Negro History. 2 volumes. Available through Pepsi-Cola. 12″ LP and filmstrip.

Afro-American Drum and Dance Ensemble: Afro-American Music in the Junior High School. MaryAnn Tyler, Pickett Middle School, Wayne and Chelten Avenues, Philadelphia, Pennsylvania. Videotape. 38 min.

American Music: From Folk to Jazz and Pop. 2 parts. McGraw-Hill Films. 51 min./black & white/sale $275/rental $25.
    An ABC-TV Project that explores the world of popular music, tracing the development of today's music to its origins in American, African and European history. The development of American jazz is explored with many of the original artists. Commentaries on jazz by notables such as Duke Ellington and Billy Taylor are included. Other streams of American music (hoedown, square dance, gospel, funeral march, etc.) are illustrated. Techniques used in the recording of popular music are given brief attention. Finally, the folk music explosion, starting in the 1960's, is ex-

plored, presenting many details of interest for students and for teachers facing the realities of today's comprehensive music classrooms.

Anacostia: Museum in the Ghetto. NET. 16mm/17 min./black & white/sale $100/rental $4.15, 1968.

Describes how a neighborhood museum, a branch of the Smithsonian Institution located in a Washington, D.C. ghetto, is bringing beauty, creativity and joy to the children there. Candid scenes depict the museum's policy of involving children in its activities. The Smithsonian's secretary and patrons of the local museum present the rationale for the museum. A youth explains why exhibits are not vandalized. Scenes of the museum's surroundings emphasize a plea for more institutions to enter the ghettos.

Black Composers and Performers Discuss Black Music. Produced under the auspices of the Black Music Seminar, Summer 1968, Dominique-René de Lerma, director. NET. 45 min./black & white, 1969.

Black musicians (Thomas Jefferson Anderson, David Baker, Natalie Hinderas, Hale Smith and Olly Wilson) discuss the problems of defining "black music."

Black Cultural Leaders in Music. George W. Jones, consulting editor. Cultural History Research, Inc., New York, N.Y. 3M International Microfilm Press, 1969.

Color filmstrip, narrated tape, microfilm resource material and teacher's guide.

Black History. Lesson 4. "The African Way of Life." Prepared by Price Cobbs and William Grier. Multi-Media Productions. 100 slides and reel-to-reel tape.

The Blues. Produced, directed and photographed by Samuel B. Charters. Distributor: Brandon Films. 21 min./color, 1963.

Color Us Black. NET. 16mm/black & white/sale $240/rental $10, 1968.

The black man's struggle for his own identity over and above the "whitey" norm is covered from the point of view of black students at predominantly black Howard University. The four-day take-over of the administration building by students seeking to overcome what they call the "irrelevant" curriculum at the University is shown, including the successful ending of the rebellion. Part of the program consists of a student-made film, wherein a black-white romantic triangle and associated problems are presented by Howard students in a freely expressed manner.

Contemporary Black Artists. (Sandak color slides, set no. 673). Sandak, Inc., 4 East 48th Street, New York, N.Y. 10017. 47 slides/color.

Consists of an exhibition of thirty contemporary black artists that was shown at the Minneapolis Institute of Arts in October 1968. The exhibition, organized in collaboration with Ruder & Finn, Inc., New York, toured major museums throughout the country. This slide set represents the exhibition that was revised during its tour. Biographical and critical commentaries prepared by Dr. Marshall W. Fishwick of Lincoln University are included free with the purchase of each complete set.

Diary of a Harlem Family. NET. 16mm/20 min./black & white/sale $125/ rental $5.50.

A poignant view of the plight of one family living in New York City's black Harlem, as seen through the photographs of Gordon Parks, the Negro writer, composer, playwright and film producer *(The Learning Tree).*

Frederick Douglass: The House on Cedar Hill. Contemporary Films. 17 min./ black & white/sale $115/rental $10.

A film on the life of Frederick Douglass (1817-1895), black leader in the struggle against slavery and its cruelties. The narrative is based on Douglass' writings, and the musical score is derived from folk songs of the black American.

Harriet Tubman and the Underground Railroad. Parts 1 and 2. McGraw-Hill Films. 54 min./black & white/sale $270/rental $15.

Produced by CBS for "The Adventure Series," this film has a cast of notables such as Ethel Waters, Ruby Dee and Ossie Davis. It portrays the first nineteen journeys Mrs. Tubman made into slave territory between 1850 and 1860.

Heritage of the Negro. NET 16mm/39 min./black & white/sale $125/rental $5.40.

Explores the heritage of the Negro by examining the civilization and achievements of ancient Africa and their significance to the American Negro today. Emphasizes that African history as recorded by white historians has traditionally ignored the old civilization of Africa below the Sahara. Explores the art, sculpture and present-day pageantry that reflect the old cultures. A film in the "History of the Negro People Series."

Jazz in the Concert Hall. McGraw-Hill Films. 15 min./black & white.

A part of the New York Philharmonic's Young People's Concert Series. Shows the fusion of jazz with classical music. Works by Schuller, Copland and Austin are performed.

The Jazz Museum Story. Produced and distributed by the New Orleans Jazz Museum, 1017 Dumaine Street, New Orleans, Louisiana 70116. 15 min./ black & white, 1965.

A survey of the evolution of jazz in the city of New Orleans.

Jazz on Campus. University of Michigan Television, 310 Mayard Street, Ann Arbor, Michigan 48104. 29 min./black & white.

A survey of several jazz styles, including modern and conventional jazz and dixieland.

Marilyn Coleman's North Philadelphia. Eastern Educational TV; Channel 12, Station WHYY-TV, 4325 Market Street, Philadelphia, Pennsylvania.

Music of Williamsburg. Modern Learning Aids. Distributors: Audio-Visual Center, Indiana University. 40 min. or 29 min./color, 1961.

Includes music of Hobart Smith, Bessie Jones, Ed Young, and the Georgia Sea Island Singers.

The Roots of American Music: The Traditional Black Blues. Washington Films. Produced by the University of Washington Archives of Ethnic Music and Dance, and the University of Washington Press, Seattle, Washington 98195. 16mm/color, February 1972.

Part 1: Performances by Jesse Fuller, Son House, Mance Lipscomb, Furry Lewis, Robert Pete Williams and John Lee Hooker. 40 min.

Part 2: Performances by Sonny Terry and Brownie McGhee, Johnny Shines, The Georgia Sea Island Singers and Jesse Fuller. 33 min.

Part 3: An extended performance by "Mississippi" Fred McDowell. 23 min.

Time to Dance. NET. 16mm/29 min./black & white/rental $5.40.

Discusses and illustrates three major forms of dance—ethnic, ballet and modern. Introduces the series of "A Time to Dance" with paintings, sculpture and film clips showing ethnic dances throughout history and the world.

Watts Towers Theatre Workshop. KCET, Los Angeles, California. 16mm/ 27 min./color/order ESC-1009/sale $240/rental $10.

The Watts Towers Theatre Workshop consists of black teenagers from the Los Angeles Watts ghetto. Through the use of improvisation techniques, the group uses everyday incidents to create a situation of active involvement, of immediate importance for personal and social change. Seen are three short acts ("Watts/Glendale," "Overdose," and

"Watermelon President") showing entertainment by, for and about people living in the ghetto. Useful for intercultural education and drama technique for secondary schools, colleges and adults.

AFRO-AMERICAN ARTISTS AND SELECTED DISCOGRAPHY

The following discography is arbitrarily divided into sections reflecting musical contributions of black Americans. The rather extensive list is provided to aid the teacher in achieving a bird's-eye view of the total historical and stylistic range of Afro-American music.

Since artists are constantly releasing new recordings and older recordings are being reissued, any discography quickly becomes obsolete. Therefore, a list of black artists with whose names and musical contributions music educators should become acquainted has been included in Appendix A, page 123. Record catalogs can be checked and recordings sampled of those artists listed.

This discography includes recordings that have proven valuable in the authors' classrooms. A few recordings have been discontinued, but most are readily accessible.

Concert Music

Composers

The Black Composer in America. Oakland Youth Orchestra, Robert Hughes, Conductor. Desto Records—DC 7107.

Ulysses Kay: "A Short Overture" (1946) is a work of contrapuntal string writing built around progressions of resonant brass chords.

George Walker: "Passacaglia" (1959) begins with an introduction leading to a "ground" over which fourteen variations are constructed.

William Grant Still: "Songs of Separation" (premiered in 1946) is based upon the lyrics of five black poets.

William Dawson: "Out in the Fields" is a setting of a poem by Imogene Guiney for soprano and orchestra.

William Fisher: "A Quiet Movement" (1966) has definite jazz overtones.

Arthur Cunningham: "Lullabye for a Jazz Baby" (1969) incorporates elements of blues and jazz.

Stephen Chambers: "Shapes for Orchestra" (1965) is a mixture of stasis and dynamism, an abstract collage of sound punctuated by granite hard, clear dissonances.

Coleridge-Taylor, Samuel (1875-1912)
　　Characteristic Waltzes (piano: arranged for orchestra). RCA Victor—
　　　　27225/6
　　The Death of Minnehaha. Columbia—C-2210-3
　　Dream Dances. Op. 74, No. 2 (piano). Decca—N-11, M-16
　　Eleanore. Columbia—DB-2083
　　Hiawatha's Wedding Feast. Gramophone—HMV C-1931-4
　　Petite Suite de Concert (London Symphony). Victor—11283/4
　　Songs of Hiawatha, No. 2, 3 & 4 (Regent Concert Orchestra). Boosey &
　　　　Hawkes—1916

Dawson, William (1899-　　)
　　Negro Folk Symphony. Decca—DL-710077
　　Spirituals. Victor—4556
　　Soon Ah Will Be Done (Roger Wagner Chorale). Capitol—P-8431

Dett, Robert Nathaniel (1882-1943)
　　In the Bottoms (piano: Natalie Hinderas). Desto—DC 7102/3
　　Spirituals. Victor—M-879
　　Adagio Cantabile (piano: Jeanne Behrend). Victor—17912
　　Listen to the Lambs (Mormon Tabernacle Choir). Philips—Nbl-5012

Handy, William Christopher (1873-1958)
　　Selected Works. Folkways—FE-3540; Capitol—SW-993
　　St. Louis Blues. RCA Victor—LPM-1714

Hayes, Roland (1887-　　)
　　Spirituals (soprano: Inez Matthews). Period—SPL-580

Kay, Ulysses Simpson (1917-　　)
　　Fantasy Variations. CRI-209
　　Sinfonia in E. CRI-139
　　Round Dance and Polka for Strings. CRI-119
　　Concerto for Orchestra. Remington Musicrama—R-199-173
　　Suite (string orchestra). LOU-634

Natalie Hinderas Plays Music by Black Composers. Desto Records—DC-
　　7102/3
　　　　A two record album of piano music by black composers.

　　R. Nathaniel Dett—"In the Bottoms" (a characteristic suite)
　　　　"In the Bottoms" is a suite in five movements:
　　　　　　Prelude: emphasis on open fifths and syncopation
　　　　　　His Song: in the style of an improvised air
　　　　　　Honey: a Negro love song

Barcarolle: the characteristic rhythmic figure of the theme of this movement is the rhythmic motif of the entire suite.

Dance (Juba): see page 101 for a classroom experience based on this dance.

William Grant Still—"Three Visions"

"Dark Horsemen" consists of a driving consistent pattern throughout.

"Summerland" is similar in quality to the composer's "Seven Traceries" and the "Songs of Separation."

"Radiant Pinnacle" is rather oriental in style, produced by augmented harmonies, pentatonic scale and a regular, flowing rhythm.

Thomas H. Kerr, Jr.—"Easter Monday Swagger: Scherzino"

Written especially for Miss Hinderas. The scherzino effect of the piece is best described in Kerr's own words as a "small filet of soul."

John W. Work—"Scuppernong"

"At a Certain Church." See page 114 for a classroom experience based on this movement.

"Ring Game." A slow movement whose theme is used to accompany a game of the Negro church.

"Visitor from Town" is reminiscent of the style of George Gershwin.

George Walker—"Piano Sonata No. 1"

The Sonata is in three movements: Allegro Energico, Theme and Variations, Allegro Con Brio. The first movement is in sonata-allegro form. It contains harmonic and melodic quartal fragments and considerable chromaticism. The first of the contrasting themes is based on a folk song found in Carl Sandburg's "Songbag." The second movement is based on the Kentucky folk song "Oh Bury Me Beneath the Willow." The third movement has a rondo-like construction.

Arthur Cunningham—"Engrams"

Mr. Cunningham describes "Engrams" thus: "I titled this piece 'Engrams' because the sounds are memory tracings. It has no time signature and was composed from a row in three forms—original, retrograde and mirror of retrograde, and adjusted to please my ear. It progresses from the dark of my mind to the light of reality."

Stephen A. Chambers—"Sound Gone"

A poetic, philosophical sketch.

Hale Smith—"Evocation"

> Mr. Smith says, "The entire piece derives from the row exposed in the first stave, and in several places has faint but definite rhythmic affinities with jazz phrasing. This doesn't mean that it's supposed to swing . . . , but the affinities are there."

Olly Wilson—"Piano Piece for Piano and Electronic Sound"

> In this piece performance on prepared strings of the piano produces unusual timbral characteristics. The piece is highly percussive, but the tape and piano sounds combine to produce melodic patterns.

Perry, Julia (1924-   )
> *Stabat Mater.* CRI-133
> *Short Piece for Orchestra.* CRI-145

Russell, George (1923-   )
> *Electronic Organ Sonata.* Flying Dutchman—122
> *Othello Ballet Suite.* Flying Dutchman—122

Smith, Hale (1925-   )
> *Contours for Orchestra.* LOU-632
> *Evocation* (piano: Natalie Hinderas). Desto—DC 7102/3
> *In Memoriam—Beryl Rubinstein* (Robert Shaw Chorale). CRI—S-182

Sowande, Fela (1905-   )
> *African Suite* (orchestra). London—LS-426
> *The Negro in the Sacred Idiom.* London—LL-533

Still, William Grant (1895-   )
> *Symphony No. 1* (Afro-American). New Records—NRLP 105
> *Symphony No. 1* (Scherzo only). Victor—2059; Columbia—11992D
> *Sahdji.* Mercury—MG-50257
> *Lennox Avenue* (blues). New Records—NRLP 105
> *From the Delta* (No. 1 Work Song). Columbia—ML 2029

Swanson, Howard (1909-   )
> *Concerto for Orchestra* (Conductor: William Steinberg). SIL—5001/2
> *Seven Songs* (Helen Thigpen). Desto—6422
> *Short Symphony.* CRI—S-254

Wilson, Olly (1937-   )
> *Piece for Four.* CRI—S-264
> *Cestus.* Turnabout—34301

Instrumentalists

Andre Watts. Columbia—MS-6636

Natalie Hinderas Plays Music by Black Composers. Desto—DC-7102/3 (see page 83 for annotation).

George Walker: Spatials; Sonata No. 2. CRI—S-270

Singers

Anderson, Marian
Farewell Recital. Victor—LSC-2781
He's Got the World (spirituals). Victor—LSC-2592

Bumbry, Grace
Arias from Verdi's "Aida." Deutsche Grammophon—DGG 138987
Brahms: Five Songs; Schubert: Five Songs; Schumann: Five Songs.
Angel—S-36454
Excerpts from Verdi's "Aida." Angel—S-36566

Hayes, Roland
Roland Hayes. Veritas—112

Matthews, Inez
Spiritual. Period—580

Maynor, Dorothy
Dorothy Maynor. Victor—LM-3086

Price, Leontyne
Arias: Puccini and Verdi. Victor—LSC-2506
Barber: "Anthony and Cleopatra." Victor—LSC-3062
Barber: "Hermit Songs." Odyssey—32160230
Bizet's "Carmen" (excerpts). Victor—LSC-2843

Robeson, Paul
Spirituals. Columbia—ML 4105
At Carnegie Hall. Vanguard—2035

Verrett, Shirley
Donizetti: "Lucrezia Borgia." Victor—LSC-6176
Spanish Songs. Victor—LSC-2776
Verdi: "La forza del destino" (excerpts). Victor—LSC-2838

Weathers, Felicia
Lieder. London—26054
Puccini and Verdi Arias. London—26014

Warfield, William
> Copland: "Old American Song." Columbia—MS 6497
> Gershwin: "Porgy and Bess" (selections). RCA—LSC-2679
> Handel: "Messiah." Columbia—M2S-603

Performing Organizations

De Paur Chorus. Mercury—90382
Fisk Jubilee Singers (Director: John Work). Folkways—FA-2372
Fisk Jubilee Singers (Director: John Work). Word Records—W-4007 LP
Tuskegee Institute Choir: Spirituals. Westminster—9633
Beverly Glenn Concert Chorale. Cross Records—LPS-333

Musical Shows

Carmen Jones. Decca—79021
Golden Boy. Capitol—SVAS-2124
Hallelujah, Baby! Columbia—KOS-3090
Hello, Dolly. RCA Victor—08S-1006
The Me Nobody Knows. Atlantic—S-1566
No Strings. Capitol—SO-1695
Original Musical Comedy: 1909-35. RCA Victor—LRV-560
Purlie. Ampex—40101

Sound Tracks

Alfie. Impulse—9111
Alice's Wonderland. Columbia—8236
Anatomy of a Murder. Columbia—1360
Blow-up. MGM—S-44447ST
The Cool World. Philips—600-138
Cotton Comes to Harlem. United Artists—5211
Elevator to the Scaffold. Columbia—1268
For Love of Ivy. ABC—OC7
In Cold Blood. Colgems—COS 107
In the Heat of the Night. United Artists—3025
The Italian Job. Paramount—5007
Jack Johnson. Columbia—30455
John and Mary. A & M Records—SP-4230
Learning Tree. Warner Brothers—S-1812
The Lost Man. UNI—73060
Man and Boy. Sussex—7011
A Milanese Story. Atlantic—1388
Mirage. Mercury—61025

Music from the Connection. Blue Note—84027
No Sun in Venice. Atlantic—1284
Odds Against Tomorrow. United Artists—4061
Paris Blues. United Artists—4092
Shaft. Enterprise—Ens-2-5002
Soul to Soul. Atlantic—SD-7207
Sweet Sweetback. Stax—Sts-3001
They Call Me Mr. Tibbs. United Artists—3045
Up Tight. Stax—2006
Zigzag. MGM—1SE21ST

Gospel

James Cleveland: God's Promises. Savoy—MG-14220
James Cleveland: Peace Be Still. Savoy—MG-14076
Reverend Gary Davis. Bluesville—LO49
Dixie Hummingbirds: Best. Peacock—8055-138M
Beverly Glenn Chorale: Coming Again So Soon. Cross Records—LPS 333
Bessie Griffin: Gospel Heart. Sunset—5195
Edwin Hawkins Singers: More Happy Days. Buddah—M85064
Mahalia Jackson: Best. Kenwood—500
Mahalia Jackson: Right Out of the Church. Columbia—CS-9813
Negro Church Music. Atlantic—1351
Art Reynolds Singers: Tellin' It Like It Is. Capitol—T 2534
Don Shirley: Gospel According to Don Shirley. Columbia—CS-9723
Ward Singers: The Famous. Savoy—4046

Blues

Anthology of Rhythm and Blues. Columbia—CS-9802
Blues Roots. Arhoolie—Poppy 60003
Ray Charles: Genius Sings the Blues. Atlantic—S-8052
Hank Crawford: Mr. Blues Plays Lady Soul. Atlantic—S-1523
W. C. Handy Blues. Folkways—FG-3540
History of Rhythm and Blues. Atlantic—8-record set
John Lee Hooker: Real Blues. Chess—1508
That's My Story: John Lee Hooker Sings the Blues. Riverside—12-321
Lightnin' Hopkins: Greatest Hits. Prestige—7592
The Legendary Son House. Columbia—CL 2414
Shaky Jake: Mouth Harp Blues. Prestige—Bluesville 1027
The Immortal Blind Lemon Jefferson. Milestone—2004
Blind Willie Johnson. Folkways—FG 3585
Robert Johnson, King of the Delta Blues Singers. Columbia—CL 1654

B. B. King: Indianola, Mississippi Seeds. ABC—S-713
Huddie Ledbetter: Keep Your Hands Off Her. Verve—FVS9021
Cripple Clarence Lofton. Vogue—LDE 122
Memphis Slim: Just Blues. Prestige—Bluesville 1018
Negro Folk Music of Alabama (game songs and others). Ethnic Folkways
    Library—4417-18, 4471-74
Negro Folklore from Texas State Prisons. Elektra—EKS-7296
Negro Folk Music of Africa and America. Folkways—FE-4500
Negro Prison Songs from the Mississippi State Penitentiary. Tradition—
    TLP 1020
Ma Rainey: Blues the World Forgot. Biograph—12001
Roots of the Blues. Atlantic—1348
Bessie Smith: Story. Columbia—CL 855-858
Bessie Smith, The World's Greatest Blues Singer. Columbia—GP 33
Roosevelt Sykes: The Honeydripper. Prestige—Bluesville 1014
Sonny Terry/Brownie McGhee. Fantasy—3254
Joe Turner: Boss of the Blues. Atlantic—1234
Dinah Washington: Best in Blues. Mercury—20247
Jimmie Witherspoon: Evenin' Blues. Prestige—7300
Muddy Waters: After the Rain. Cadet—CS-320
Nancy Wilson: Hurt So Bad. Capitol—ST353
Howlin' Wolf: Moanin' in the Moonlight. Chess—1434
Women of the Blues. RCA Victor—LPV 534
Jimmie and Mama Yancey: Pure Blues. Atlantic—1283

Jazz

Gene Ammons: Blue Gene. Prestige—7146
Louis Armstrong Story. Columbia—CL 851-854
The Art of Jazz Piano (James P. Johnson and others). Epic—LN 3295
Albert Ayler: Trio. ESP—1002
Basie's Best. Decca—DXB 170S 7170
Count Basie: Essential. Verve—8407
Birth of Big Band Jazz (Henderson, Ellington, et al.). Riverside—129
The Eighty-Six Years of Eubie Blake. Columbia—C 23847
Eubie Blake: Wizard of Ragtime Piano. 20th Century Fox (A)—3003
Eubie Blake: The Marches I Played on the Old Ragtime Piano. 20th Century
    Fox (A)—3039
Art Blakey: African Beat. Blue Note—4097
Donald Byrd: Fancy Free. Blue Note—84319
Charlie Christian with the Goodman Sextet. Columbia—CL 652
Ornette Coleman: Shape of Jazz to Come. Atlantic—1317

Ornette Coleman: This Is Our Music. Atlantic—S-1353
John Coltrane: Avant-Garde (with Don Cherry). Atlantic—1451
John Coltrane: Live at the Village Vanguard. Impulse—A10
Ken Colyer: They All Played Ragtime. Decca (E)—DFE6466
Creative Ragtime. Euphonic (A)—CSR-1206
Miles Davis: Birth of the Cool. Capitol—T-762
Miles Davis: Bitches Brew. Columbia—GP 26
Miles Davis: In a Silent Way. Columbia—CS 9875
Miles Davis: Jack Johnson. Columbia—S-30455
Miles Davis - Gil Evans: Porgy and Bess. Columbia—CL 1274
Miles Davis: Quiet Nights. Columbia—CL 2106
Duke Ellington: Indispensable. RCA Victor—LPM 6009
Music of Duke Ellington. Columbia—CL 558
Bill Evans: Trio 64. Verve—68578
Ella Fitzgerald: Ella and Basie. Verve—68683
Giants of Boogie-Woogie (Meade Lux Lewis and others). Riverside—12106
Dizzie Gillespie: Greatest. RCA Victor—LPM 2398
Golden Age of Ragtime. Riverside (A)—12-110
Herbie Hancock: Maiden Voyage. Blue Note—84195
Coleman Hawkins: Documentary. Riverside—117/8
Coleman Hawkins: Genius (with Oscar Peterson). Verve—8261
Heliotrope Bouquet (Piano Rags 1900-1970), William Bolcom, piano. None-
    such—H-71257
History of Jazz: The New York Scene. Folkways—2823
Billie Holiday: Lady Day. Columbia—CL 637
Jazz. 2 volumes. Folkways—2801-2811
Jazz: Volume V (Chicago No. 1). Folkways—2805
Bunk Johnson. Columbia (E)—33SX 1015
James P. Johnson. Extra (E)—1024
James P. Johnson, Father of Stride Piano. Columbia—CL 170
Piano Rags by Scott Joplin (Joshua Rifkin, piano). Nonesuch—H-71248
Scott Joplin: Ragtime Pioneer (1899-1914). Riverside—8815
Joplin, Turpin, et al. Riverside (A)—12-126
Louis Jordan's Greatest Hits. Decca—DL 75035
Lee Konitz: Meets Mulligan. Pacific Jazz—38
Lee Konitz: Subconscious—Lee. Prestige—7250
Joseph Lamb. Folkways (A)—3562
Yusef Lateef: Eastern Sounds. Prestige—MVLP 22 A
Jazz Abstractions: John Lewis Presents Contemporary Music. Atlantic—SD
    1365
Charles Lloyd: Forest Flower. Atlantic—1473

Jimmie Lunceford and His Orchestra. Decca—DL 8050
Charlie Mingus: Mingus, Mingus, Mingus. Impulse—A 54
Charlie Mingus: Pithecanthropus Erectus. Atlantic—1237
Modern Jazz Quartet with Jimmy Giuffre: Django. Prestige—7057
Third Stream Music: Modern Jazz Quartet and Guests. Atlantic—SD1345
Jelly Roll Morton. Library of Congress Recordings
Jelly Roll Morton: Classic Piano. Riverside—111
The King of New Orleans Jazz, Jelly Roll Morton. RCA Victor—LPM 1649
Thelonius Monk: Monk's Moods. Prestige—7159
King Oliver's Dixie Syncopators. Ace of Hearts—AH 34
King Oliver in New York. RCA Victor—LPV 529
Charlie Parker: Essential. Verve—68409
Charlie Parker: Greatest Recording Session (with Miles Davis). Savoy—12079
Amazing Bud Powell. Blue Note—1503-1504
Bud Powell Trio. Fantasy—86006
Ragtime Piano Roll (Joplin, et al.). 4 volumes. Riverside (A) RLB-1006, 1025,
    1040, 1060
Sonny Rollins: Saxophone Colossus. Prestige—7079
George Russell Sextet: Stratusphunk. Riverside—RIP 341
Solar Sun Ra and His Arkestra: Heliocentric Worlds. ESP—1014
Ralph Sutton: Backroom Piano. Columbia (E)—33 CX 10061
The Essential Art Tatum. Verve—68433
Clark Terry: Color Changes. Candid—8009 9009
Three Decades of Jazz (1939-69). Blue Note—89902/3/4
Lennie Tristano: Lennie. Atlantic—1224
Sarah Vaughan: Sings Gershwin. Mercury—60045-6
Fats Waller and His Rhythm. RCA Victor—LPM 1503
The Real Fats Waller. RCA Camden—473
Gerald Wilson: Eternal Equinox. Pacific Jazz—20160
Lester Young: At His Very Best. Emarcy—66010
Lester Young: Pres. Verve—8162

Soul

Birth of Soul (Armstrong, Fitzgerald, Holiday, Tharpe, Jordan, B. Johnson,
    Hampton, et al.). An anthology. Decca—79245
James Brown: Ain't It Funky. King Records—KS 1092
James Brown: Handful of Soul. Smash Records—67084
James Brown: The Popcorn. King Records—S-1055
The Chambers Brothers: The Time Has Come. Columbia—CL 2722
Ray Charles: Crying Time. ABC—S-744
Ray Charles: Man and His Soul. 2-ABC—S-590X

Ray Charles: Recipe for Soul. ABC—S-465
The Nat King Cole Trio. Capitol—T 3311
Roberta Flack: First Take. Atlantic—S-8230
Aretha Franklin: Aretha's Gold. Atlantic—S-8227
Isaac Hayes: Hot Buttered Soul. Enterprise—1001
Isaac Hayes: To Be Continued. Enterprise—1014
Jimi Hendrix: Are You Experienced? Reprise—M86261
Jimi Hendrix: Bold As Love. Reprise—M86281
Hoodoo Man Blues. Delmark—DS 9612
ABC Jackson Five. Motown—MS 709
Grits Ain't Groceries (Little Milton). Checker—LPA 3011
Lou Rawls Live. Capitol—ST-2459
Otis Redding: Dictionary of Soul. Atco—S-33-249
Smokey Robinson and the Miracles. Tamla—276
Nina Simone: Let It All Out. Philips—600202
Sly and the Family Stone. Epic—KE 30325
Johnny Taylor. Stax—STS 2012
The Temptations. Gordy—D.S. 954

CLASSROOM EXPERIENCES

The goals of presenting the following material are: first, to help student and teacher grow in sensitiveness to the unique qualities of Afro-American music, i.e., to help them grow in knowledge, feelingfulness and skills relevant to the Afro-American experience; and, second, to motivate new and deeper insights into the experience of the black man and his style of producing and consuming "black music."

A byproduct of pursuing such goals would be the development of individuals who are open to change, adaptive and flexible, respectful of differences, able to learn continuously, and who constructively meet new and challenging aesthetic problems.

Rhythmic concepts were chosen as the focus for most of the following classroom experiences. The suggested experiments are intended as exemplars of curricular strategies utilizing Afro-American music and as points of departure for continued experimentation by the teacher. Each stated experience and the suggested experiments reinforce the belief that the elements of sound are the bridge by which one gains an understanding of music of diverse styles and cultures. It is the study of the various possibilities of *organization* and *interaction* of these elements that helps to close the gap of understanding in examining the many musical traditions prevalent in our environment.

Experience I.

Assisting the ear and the mind to become sensitive to musical motion.

In this experience students will be guided to discover that musical motion can range in speed from extremely slow to extremely fast, and that there are other speeds such as moderately slow or moderately fast which fall somewhere in between the extremes.

1. Have students tap lightly to their heartbeat. Experiment with altering the rate of the heartbeat by jogging in place or by recording the heartbeat on tape and then changing speeds. Ask individual students to add complementary rhythmic patterns.

2. Using the taped patterns from the experiences in No. 1, have students identify the heartbeat and use it as a pulse for other complementary rhythmic patterns. Select a song or poem to perform with one of these patterns. Experiment by varying rhythm, timbre and density.

3. Demonstrate the metronome. Discuss the differences and similarities between the metronome beat and the heartbeat. Show how this mechanical tool can indicate different speeds exactly by having selected students tap tempo terms (*allegro, largo,* etc.) indicated by the metronome.

4. Discuss rhythmic limitations and advantages of a mechanical tempo-setting device. Have students perform along with recorded examples of soul music, keeping a metronome-set tempo throughout. Have them perform the same song without the metronome. Discuss differences and similarities, advantages and disadvantages observed.

Did the students discover that—

. . . a mechanical device, however useful, cannot reflect or meet the needs of the myriad range of "life movements and feelings of movement"?

. . . the heartbeat—being a part of us—changes in tempo in response to how we feel about life around us?

. . . making decisions regarding how fast or how slow a composition should go is made easier when one is familiar with an entire piece —the "insides" and the "outsides"; also, the "sense of time" with which all of us are born—in varying degrees—determines our skill in making tempo decisions that are successful and unique?

Experience II.

Assisting the eye and ear in the identification of aural and written rhythmic patterns.

1. Put various rhythmic patterns on a chalkboard or overhead projector. Clap them as students observe and listen. Number each pattern. Have students identify the pattern clapped. The student's task is to match written symbols to the sound heard. All patterns can be performed singly or together. Numbers can be substituted for notes, using "x" to indicate a rest, as follows.

2. Have students perform the following patterns, reading from the chalkboard or overhead projector.

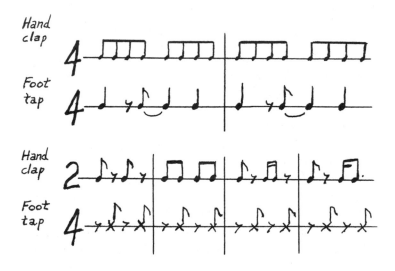

3. Select individual students to clap each of the following patterns. See if other students can identify the pattern clapped. Have all students perform

the patterns. Indicate individual patterns to be performed as a means of testing the students. After patterns are mastered, divide the class into four or more sections and have them perform the patterns together. Obtain a variety of timbre by using student-suggested techniques for sound production. Have individual students take turns improvising on any basic beat pattern.

4. Create (improvise) additional patterns to add to the following.

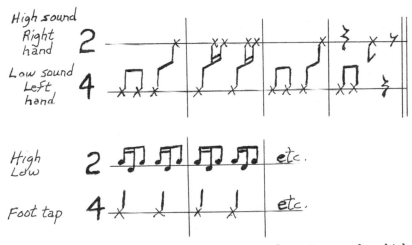

5. Direct students to read rhythmic patterns by using words which are rhythmically similar to the pattern.

Jump to the beat

6. Have students symbolize and clap the rhythm of individual names.

short - short - long - long - long

John-ny Boy Jack-son

7. Ask students to respond to various tempi by performing designated note patterns at various speeds.

8. Have students clap characteristic rhythmic patterns of various currently popular dances.

9. Select a syllable and have students chant selected rhythmic patterns (or new but related patterns) from the above experiences. Four patterns may be selected and performed as a round. Have students perform the round in a "follow the leader" fashion after instructing the leader to vary the tempo (and timbre and/or related expressive devices) as desired.

10. Have students perform the round discussed in No. 9 on various rhythm instruments. Encourage improvised versions of this pattern. Through the addition of instruments, the concepts of texture and timbre may be reinforced. Have students listen to the final section (prior to the percussion ending) of "Walk on By" (Isaac Hayes. *Hot Buttered Soul*. Enterprise—1001; see pages 98 and 105 for further use of this piece). Note the changes of timbre and texture achieved through the addition of instruments in repetitions of the same pattern.

11. Have students discover and discuss the expressive values and potentials (or lack of them) of thickening or thinning instrumentation in relation to various tempo settings.

12. Have students compare various recordings (to include different arrangements) of the same composition to illustrate different interpretations of tempo terms indicated in scores.

13. Divide students into small "activity sections" (groups of three to four). Have them, by clapping, singing, and performing on instruments, interpret the expressive terms given in a selected composition. Lead them to discover that, from written music, the performer must constantly make decisions as to

how fast or slow a piece should be performed, or how much tempo variation (such as rubato) should be applied.

14. Help the class translate the given note values of the Experience II experiments into new symbols, syllables or any other appropriate form of notation or rhythmic indications.

Did the students discover that—

> . . . patterns when combined are sometimes easier to read and perform than a single pattern? Why is this?
>
> . . . two or more timbres used with the same pattern seem to affect the rhythmic feeling of that pattern? For example, lower and thicker sounds followed by higher and thinner sounds, or vice versa, seem to cause a "bending" or some kind of altering of the basic rhythm.

Experience III.

Directed listening as a means of helping students understand the constant processes of acculturation, cross-influence and assimilation in music produced and consumed by the Afro-American.

1. Have students listen to John Coltrane's *Kulu Sé MaMa* (Impulse—AS-9106). Compare it with examples of African music.

Kulu Sé MaMa is an intentional attempt by Coltrane, in collaboration with Juno Lewis, to merge elements of contemporary jazz techniques with its African roots. The presentation is intentionally trance-like and ritualistic. Contributing to the ritualistic nature, the singing and much of the playing by the horns produce the cadences of a chant. At times the piece provides an insistent six-beat grouping, with strong pulses falling occasionally on 1 and 4. There is much diversity of rhythmic texture and tone quality. Juno Lewis' singing in this recording has the character of an Afro-Creole dialect which he cites as Entobes. His drums include the *juolulu*, water drums and the *doom dahka*. Other instruments used are the bells (gong-gongs), conch shell, *mbira*, saxophones, piano and bass.

Have students identify the following important musical characteristics:
> a. Saxophones in dissonant harmonies
> b. Polyphonic textures
> c. Individual treatment of musical lines
> d. "Moaning sax," later imitated by conch shell
> e. Rhythmic ostinato
> f. Piano solo using atonal harmonies
> g. Irregular and conflicting meters
> h. "Horn call" in sax and conch shell

Describe the timbres heard at the end of the composition. How does this music compare with that of contemporary composers such as Bartók, Webern, Schoenberg or Cage.

Construct a chart designating places where the following events occur: cymbal crash, loud drum roll, other percussion *ad lib.*, eventually leading to—

Voice (chant-like) *Mbira*	}	soft? loud? rhythmically free? strict?
Voice Cymbal Rattle	}	soft? loud? played in what way?
Voice more melodic Other tone colors	}	clashing sounds? pulse strong? weak? accents regular? shifting? cross-rhythms? no cross-rhythms?

Listen again to discover and designate other musical events.

2. Have students discuss what makes a particular composition "black." Using the following "Design for Listening," * motivate students to isolate those components they deem uniquely black in Isaac Hayes' arrangement and rendition of the Burt Bacharach tune, "Walk on By."

Design for Listening (on page 99)
"Walk on By"
(Isaac Hayes. *Hot Buttered
Soul.* Enterprise—1001)

---

* The "Design for Listening" is a means of motivating new and, with repeated listenings, more subtle musical discoveries. It is a means of developing the capacity to describe sound phenomena as they occur in time. The numbers represent a sequence of musical events. Students as they listen can call the numbers at the appropriate times, or they can merely follow along with the sequence of musical events described. Students should be encouraged to alter these descriptions according to their own discoveries.

This listening technique was developed in a project directed by Bennett Reimer, entitled "Development and Trial in a Junior and Senior High School of a Two-Year Curriculum in General Music." Washington, D.C.: U.S. Department of Health, Education and Welfare, Office of Education, 1967.

Events

1   Introduction: drums; orchestra, strings prominent; voices; percussion background; accented beats $1 + \hat{2} + 1 + \hat{2} +$ etc. . . . Strong, accented ending.

2   Fuzzbox guitar (electric) "reciting"; voice interruption: "walk . . . walk!"

3   Vamp; guitar and percussion.

4   Electric guitar improvises; percussion and bass background. Electronic effects: sliding, stretched sounds; all strings slide downward.

5   Repeat of No. 1: fuzzbox guitar . . . repetitious, high pitched note added.

6   Man's voice: "If you see . . . walk on by." Ensemble accompanies.

7   Female voices join male soloist; strings high pitched, prominent; strings sustain pitch.

8   Female voices: "ah" (same pitch harmonized in strings (No. 7). Soloist continues. . . .

9   Bridge material: thick chords.

10   Repeat of No. 2 and No. 5; soloist hums; guitar; flute descends, then trills.

11   Soloist: "I just can't get over you . . . ;" flute; guitar; ensemble accompanies; percussion beats $1 + \hat{2} + 1 + \hat{2} +$; flute prominent.

12   Female voices and soloist; strings smooth in high register; strong accents; strings sustain pitch (similar to No. 7).

13   Repeat of No. 8; female voices: "ah"—string pitch of No. 7 harmonized.

14   Man's voice sings on . . .; "Oh momma". . . .
Female voices:

              oboe melody   oboe melody   oboe melody
    "walk on"   "walk on"   "walk on"

15   Orchestra: brasses prominent—ascending; gets thicker, louder. Strings prominent and descend with strong accent (as in No. 1).

Repeat piece from Event No. 10. Notice differences in music, text, dynamics, or use of instruments. Compare the Hayes version with that of Dionne Warwick (*Walk On By*, Scepter Records—S-WF-21029).

Did the students discover that—

... the stressed beat is 2 rather than 1?

... there are "call and response" techniques?

... the creative "bending" of typically European musical traditions and techniques is appropriate to the needs of the "soul" techniques of the black performer?

3. Have students listen to and compare Isaac Hayes' version of "By the Time I Get to Phoenix" (in *Hot Buttered Soul*. Enterprise—1001) with the one by Glen Campbell, a white performer *(By the Time I Get to Phoenix*. Capitol—ST-2851).

The black performer makes a rendition strikingly "black" by bringing himself and the black experience to that rendition. An excellent example of this is illustrated in a great deal of popular and folk music written by whites and performed by blacks. Isaac Hayes' rendition of "By the Time I Get to Phoenix" is a superb example of this.

"By the Time I Get to Phoenix" is a *tour de force* of approximately eighteen minutes, including the more than ten-minute monologue (quasi-sermon) that includes such effects as moans, grunts, wails, shouts, gliding pitches, and song-speech. Hayes is actually telling a story, a kind of soliloquy dramatizing the story of a heartbroken man trying to leave a woman who has taken him for a fool. The "soulful" manner in which the story is told is uniquely black, and as Phyl Garland, the black authoress, says, it is truly "somethin' else."

During this soliloquy, Hayes merely strikes a basic chord on the organ and sustains it against a rhythmic background. Comparing this rendition with that of Glen Campbell can prove highly instructive in considering the black experience and its influence on what can happen to music composed by a white person but re-created with the freedom, skill and naturalness of an accomplished black soul singer. Further, a closer scrutiny of these two versions can reveal much about the acculturation and assimilation process constantly working in reciprocity with blacks and whites in America.

4. Have students listen to and sing the Osmond Brothers single "One Bad Apple" (MGM—S 4724). Are performance techniques employed that give a flavor of what one might call black music? Can students suggest any other examples of "mutual assimilation" in music? How does the sound of this group compare to that of the Jackson Five *(Diana Ross Presents Jackson Five*. Motown—MO S 700)?

Have students clap while singing "One Bad Apple." What is the meter? What beats are stressed? Listen to Hayes' "Walk on By" (see pages 96 and 98). Are there differences in beat, tempo, style? Try playing the Hayes piece on 45 rpm instead of 33⅓. Compare the meter and rhythmic stresses with those in the Osmond Brothers performance.

5. Have the students examine and respond to examples of concert music written by black composers; help them to discover those characteristics and elements that resisted assimilation and those that are explainable in terms identified with Western art music. The following activities relate to Nathaniel Dett's "Juba Dance" (*Natalie Hinderas Plays Music by Black Composers.* Desto Records—DC-7102/3).

"Pattin' a juba" is the stamping on the ground with the foot and following it with two staccato pats of the hands in duple meter. In the early days, among blacks, at least one-third of the dancers kept time in this way, while the others danced. Sometimes the dancers would combine to urge a solo dancer on to more frantic maneuvers. The orchestra usually consisted of a single fiddler perched high on a box or table and who, forgetful of self in the hilarious excitement of the hour, exhibited virtuosic technique in double stopping and bowing.

Have students clap and stamp this juba pattern ("pattin' a juba") while chanting, then improvise additional rhythmic patterns.

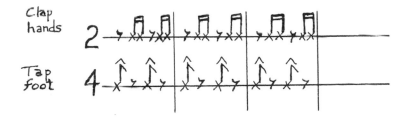

Listen to the Hinderas rendition of "Juba Dance"; encourage students to learn the two basic melodies. Ask them to clap the juba pattern (above) on the second or third time through. Have the students pay close attention not only to the sounds produced but also to any physical movements that are suggested when these sounds are produced.

Ask students if they know the rhythm game called hambone. If so, have them perform it. How does it relate to "pattin' a juba"? Does either the juba or the hambone feel more natural if the rhythmic patterns are prepared mentally and physically from *motion*, instead of only musically, from hearing? Experiment with these possibilities.

Encourage students to discover the main sections of "Juba Dance," identifying the patterns of the music and the dance. Repeat the piece and help them discover the smaller phrase patterns; you may use the diagram shown below (draw it on the chalkboard without the letters and have students indicate when each part begins, changes and returns). Have them suggest descriptive names or symbols for both the closing section and the "key-change" section.

Where do these melodies occur?

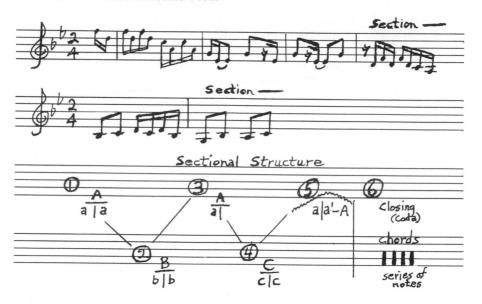

Assign numbers representing each section to each student; play the "Juba Dance" again and suggest that each number be called just prior to its entrance. Other students can call out the number if the student forgets or proves insecure or inaccurate.

Compare this piano version of "Juba Dance" with an orchestral version (RCA Victor *Record Library for Elementary Schools*, Volume 6, 45-5023-A). What differences are observed? Which version is preferred and why?

Did the students discover—

    . . . the rhythm pattern of the *B* melody and the repeated-note pattern and its consequent ascending scale passage in the *B* section? Relate this instrumental "question-answer" technique to the vocal "call and response" technique.

    . . . that the ways in which their hands and feet moved reflected both the music and how they felt about it?

    . . . that there are changes in mode?

In the whole of Experience III did students also discover that—

. . . a mutual acculturation, cross-influence, even assimilation in the black and white music of the United States have taken place?

. . . sound, manipulated by the skillful musician, is an excellent carrier of social changes and of forces which cause these changes?

. . . the performer can do a great deal to make a particular piece of music sound "black" or "white"?

. . . various words and word usage (insofar as we have been conditioned in our culture) contribute to experiences with and view of music of different cultures?

. . . acculturation refers to the changes in the cultural patterns of people who have come into continuous contact with groups of different cultural orientation?

Experience IV.

Gaining a sense of syncopation by deliberately altering the expected accents.

1. Ask students to try the following methods of altering or "bending" the usual accents of meters indigenous to Western music in which one finds a regularly recurring accent on the first beat of note groupings. Create your own "syncopated" patterns.

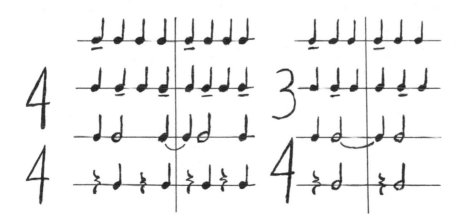

2. While clapping the top line of the following example, have students count the numbers quietly to help them "get" the beat and begin to "feel" the sense of the beat.

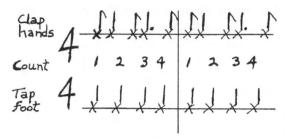

Divide the class into two parts. Clap and tap both parts, then ask for words or syllables which could be chanted to the combined rhythms. Have students chant softly and listen to themselves, noting the intriguing rhythmic irregularities.

3. Carrying the second experiment a step further, have students perform the following pattern. The underlying pulse is notated on the top line, while the irregular pattern is given on the bottom line. After getting the feel of these shifting accents, have individual students improvise similar rhythmic patterns.

4. Have students reinforce concepts developed thus far by involving them with creative uses of the accent (see next example). Experiment with other accented and syncopated patterns in this and other meters.

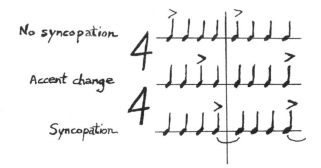

No syncopation

Accent change

Syncopation

5. Have students listen to the percussion ending of Isaac Hayes' recording of "Walk on By" (see page 98). They will hear a regular beat pattern, played on a high-hat cymbal, combined with a pattern that contradicts the meter. Ask students to improvise other syncopated patterns.

6. Involve students in singing spirituals. Select those with continuous syncopated patterns, if possible, especially those having dotted-note patterns or triplet figures. Have students first clap the rhythm of the melody, then chant the words in rhythm. Be especially careful with any triplets and dotted-note patterns. Look for any "disturbed" pulse, that which seems to contradict the underlying pulse and established rhythmic pattern.

7. The following experiment, "The Strength of the Weak Beat," * can provide ample opportunity for improvisation and group movement. By counting 1 + 2 + 3 + 4 + throughout, have students figure out the rhythmic patterns. Try clapping first, then use, perhaps, a conga drum. The suggested grouping of these numbers may help. Each pattern should begin several measures after the previous one begins.

---

* An activity conceived by the Stoddart-Fleisher Uzuri Ensemble, a group of junior high school students from Philadelphia. The patterns, emphasizing the weak beat, represent the percussion accompaniment to an Afro-American dance created by this group.

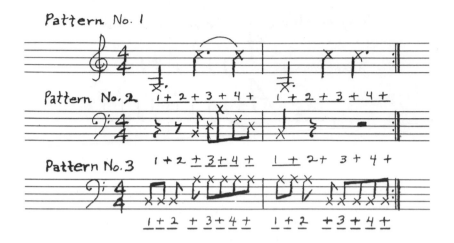

Discuss the notated pitches; they are intended to be only approximate. By dragging your arm or hand across the drum skin you can produce the approximate pitch differences indicated. Strike the drum head with one hand while making a dragging motion with the other. Experiment with different sounds by striking the conga drum also on its body. Note the characteristics of the timbre resulting from the combining of these patterns. Use your own symbols to portray visually the sound that occurs from performing the above three patterns.

8. Have students listen to Santana's *Waiting* (Columbia—CS-0781). Identify any relationships between this piece and the patterns presented in Experiment No. 7.

While listening, students should count 1 - 2 - 3 - 4 - 5 - 6 - 7 - 8 to coincide with the musical patterns. Note the metrical overlap (heard on a drum) in Event No. 3, measure 2, beat 5. This overlap produces a subtle disturbance in the sequence of events, but is usually not perceived on the first hearing.

Events

1	Bongo begins basic rhythmic pattern. Students should count the numbers in each "measure."	12345678/12345678
2	Bass with abbreviated version of first pattern.	12345678/12345678
3	Drums with another variation.	12345678/12345678

4   Timbale with a third variation.   12345678/12345678/12345678

5

6   (Continue by identifying other events.)

9. The following are basic jazz rhythms. In the first example note that the first pattern has the feel of four plus three beats. The second example has been divided into three plus four. While this pattern can be executed by one player, we suggest that one student be assigned to each part.
     Change these patterns to include syncopated effects.

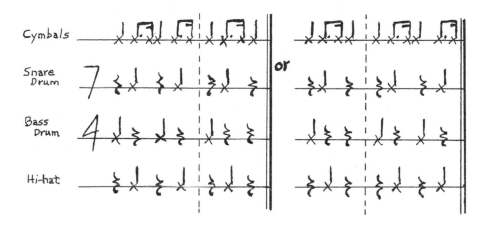

10. This pattern is found in Dave Brubeck's "Take Five" (Time Out. Columbia—CS8192). Dividing composite meters such as this into its component simple meters (3 + 2 or 2 + 3) is common in jazz. Develop accompaniment patterns to this basic rhythm.

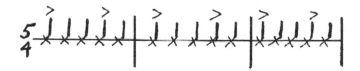

11. A simple change in the division of the beats in a composite meter can cause a striking disturbance in rhythmic pulse. Try the following pattern found in Brubeck's "Blue Rondo a la Turk" (Time Out. Columbia—CS8192). The contrast should be apparent between the 2 + 2 + 2 + 3 grouping of the ⅜ time signature and that of the 3 + 3 + 3 (the usual ⅜ division). This is an

excellent example of syncopation often found in jazz. Clap the patterns, moving the entire body to experience the *feel* of the rhythm.

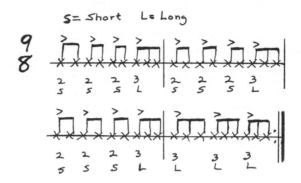

12. Now listen to Brubeck's "Unsquare Dance" *(Time Further Out.* Columbia—CS8490). Have the students identify the meter, divide it into beat groupings (as in Experiments 8-10) and symbolize (notate) the result. Discuss elements of syncopation that exist in this piece.

13. Listen to "Oh Happy Day" (Quincy Jones' *Walking in Space.* A&M— SP 3023). Lead students to discover the syncopated patterns.

Have students tap the pulse lightly on their desks throughout one or two of the sections represented in the following "Design for Listening."

Design for Listening
"Oh Happy Day"
(Quincy Jones. *Walking in
Space.* A & M—SP 3023)

Events

1   Bass guitar, beat 1 2 3 4 / 1 2 3 4, etc., electric piano, rhythm guitar and drums in background anticipate entry of melody in No. 2.

2   Flute begins melody (legato); other instruments continue softly in background. Note this pattern:

3   Voices enter with "Oh Happy Day" four times over other instruments. Strong pulse; accents.

4   Strong accent leads to brass *ff*, with blaring voices in long notes; loud, fast moving bass guitar; accents; strong pulse; pause.

5   Flute with legato melody as in No. 2. Soft voices in background; the rhythmic pattern notated in No. 2 predominates.

6   Strong accent leads to reentry of brass *ff* with blaring voices in long notes; fast moving bass in background.

7   Flute trill; legato melody in flute (now higher in pitch); instrumental accompaniment; subdued voices repeating "Oh Happy Day"; fade out.

Ask students to improvise a rhythmic pattern using the strong, regular beat of this tune as the basic pulse. Encourage students to sing the melody or to harmonize with the music played on the recording. As with any listening experience, this one may be extended to include considerations of elements other than rhythm.

Did the students discover that—

. . . syncopation (a deliberate upsetting of the normal pulse) results when a stress occurs on a beat that normally would not be stressed, or if an accent is removed from a beat where it would normally be expected?

. . . a deviation from a system of musical rhythm involving the grouping of equal beats into patterns of twos or threes, with a periodic accent on the first beat of each group, is felt as conflict, disturbance, or even contradiction between the meter and the actual rhythm?

. . . Negro spirituals are unique for their frequent use of syncopation?

. . . syncopation also can occur (and is often most striking) when there is a unique subdivision of beats?

. . . stressing the weaker beats can result in unusual and very striking patterns of notes of equal durations?

. . . while a superior sense of time makes it easier for one to grasp even some of the most difficult syncopated patterns, our rhythmic abilities can be sharpened through systematic study, attentive listening, and feelingful reaction?

. . . the common method of causing syncopation is shifting an accent to the normally weak beats by using rests where strong beats normally occur or by sustaining tones through a strong beat?

. . . "things" happen to rhythm in African and Afro-American music which upset or disturb the underlying pulse or rhythm but that cannot be explained by the traditional definition of syncopation?

. . . the effect of syncopation can be lost if the ear accepts the unequal divisions or irregular accents as a natural expectation? An effective use of syncopation occurs when one uses it judiciously, to create a shock effect. Many jazz styles, however, employ syncopated effects more frequently, even continuously, as in ragtime, yet the style of ragtime causes the ear to accept the constant syncopation, particularly when not performed too fast.

14. This activity explores the possibilities of ragtime as a serious form of composition. Examples from *Heliotrope Bouquet (Piano Rags 1900-1970)* (Nonesuch—H-71257) will be discussed and partially analyzed, providing a bird's-eye view of the technique of leading originators of piano rags. Since a major feature of ragtime is a syncopated rhythm, students should use the knowledge gained in previous experiments presented in Experience IV in describing musical events occurring in ragtime.

The analysis and discussion of this music should prove helpful not only in directing attention to specific musical happenings in ragtime music, but should also motivate additional searches into the more subtle aspects of "ragging." This, in turn, may lead to a more open attitude toward the aesthetic experiences that can be derived from the music of this unique style.

Heliotrope Bouquet (Piano Rags 1900-1970)

Side 1

Band 1—"A Rag-time Nightmare" (March and Two-Step), 1900, by Tom Turpin (1873-1922).

Indicate the moment when each of the following musical events occurs: Introduction: (diminished chords — *ff*)

1 2 1 2 (scalar figure) 1 2 1 2 (scalar figure)

A
A } Primarily scalewise

B
B } Primarily chordal—many strong accents

C
C } (Trio) scalewise—repeated in higher register

B
B } Primarily chordal—many strong accents

Listen to the composition several times, adding other descriptions (use words or symbols of your choice) of musical events heard.

Band 2—"The Easy Winners" (A Rag Time Two-Step), 1901, by Scott Joplin (1868-1917).

This rag consists of strong and easily recognized contrasts among its parts. Chordal content contrasts with the melodic scalar passages. It is moderate in tempo with a typical two-step swing. The contrapuntal dissonances and chromatic passing tones give the piece its character. As is true with a great number of rags, there is strong contrast between the left hand bass pattern and the material of the right hand. Describe what you hear in these two contrasting parts.

Band 3—"Heliotrope Bouquet" (A Slow Drag Two-Step), 1907, by Scott
          Joplin and Louis Chauvin (1883-1908).
Opens with a syncopated rhythmic scalar pattern typical of rags:

Joplin wrote down the first two strains of the piece while Chauvin played; the remainder of the piece was conceived by Joplin. One can distinguish the strains belonging to Chauvin, a Creole, by the impressionistic sounds which contrast with Joplin's clear and more straightforward harmonies of the last two strains. After listening, identify that material which is by Joplin and that by Chauvin. Describe the differences observed.

Band 5—"Pegasus" (A Classic Rag), 1919, by James Scott (1886-1936).
While listening to these two rags (Bands 4 and 5), determine if the following techniques typical of "ragging" are present:
    a. The duple meter and jagged rhythm patterns such as:

    b. A seemingly continuous syncopated rhythm.
    c. A regular and persistent (almost march-like) pattern played in the
       left hand or lower piano register, presenting a full sound in a
       kind of om-pah rhythm.

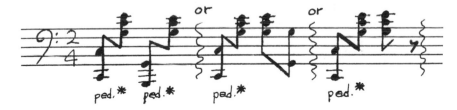

111

d. The right hand, also highly rhythmic, devoted to the primary melody.

e. A seemingly improvised sound (although early ragtime is basically notated music).

f. A discernible form, often utilizing three or four equally important tunes or strains.

Side 2

Band 5—"Brass Knuckles," 1969, by William Albright (1944-) and William Bolcom (1938-).

This unusual rag is said to have been written partly as a musical joke, as an antidote to the delicate rags the two composers were creating at the time. The score contains markings like "Brutal!"—"Loutish!"—"Dust Your Knuckles!" The piece includes numerous dissonant chord crashes, strong accents, abrupt key changes, strong contrasts between upper and lower registers of piano and much contrary motion. The musical design is as follows:

Introduction — very dissonant, crashing clusters (*ff*) in a somewhat "crazy" pattern of movement.

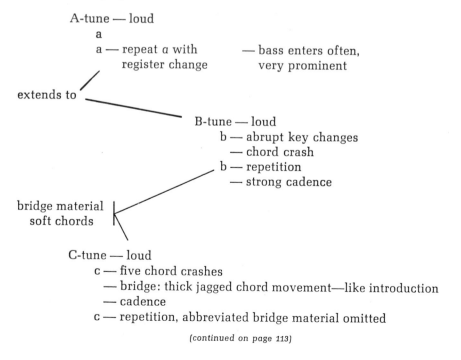

A-tune — loud
  a
  a — repeat *a* with   — bass enters often,
      register change   very prominent

extends to

                    B-tune — loud
                      b — abrupt key changes
                        — chord crash
                      b — repetition
                        — strong cadence

bridge material
  soft chords

    C-tune — loud
      c — five chord crashes
        — bridge: thick jagged chord movement—like introduction
        — cadence
      c — repetition, abbreviated bridge material omitted

(continued on page 113)

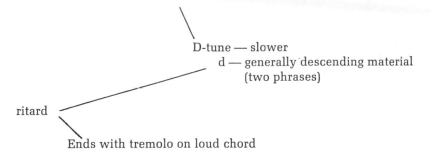

D-tune — slower

d — generally descending material
(two phrases)

ritard

Ends with tremolo on loud chord

Listen to "Brass Knuckles" (without the aid of the above chart) or other rags and do the following:

   a. Indicate the various parts heard (such as A – B – A or A – C – C). Use letters or symbols of your choice.

   b. Diagram the design of the composition in terms of dynamic levels: loud, soft, loud; *ff – pp, ff, p;* or

   c. Describe the design of the composition in terms of meter, meter changes and tempo; for example:

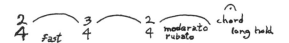

   d. Compare your descriptions with that given in the above chart.

15. Play examples of the ragtime music of Eubie Blake, Tom Turpin, James P. Johnson, Scott Joplin, Joseph Lamb, James Scott, Ralph Sutton, and others, as listed in the Jazz Discography, page 89. This music presents an excellent view of early ragtime and its extension into "stride" piano of Harlem (New York).

Students should be urged to listen critically, concentrating on both the music and its performance to gain an understanding of ragtime. Since the roots of jazz are in ragtime, special attention should be given to its influence on later trends in jazz.

A class project could involve each student in researching and reporting on selected recordings and/or articles on ragtime. Lead students to discover and become increasingly sensitive to the layers of rhythmic patterns and syncopated motion.

Experience V.

Freeing the mind and body from a feeling of strict duple or triple meter and of regularly recurring accents.

1. In performing the following example, sense the freedom and rhythmic interest motivated by the combining of these rhythmic patterns:

2. Use various timbres in combining the following patterns. For example, stamp *a* while tapping *b* and *c* with left and right fingertips respectively.

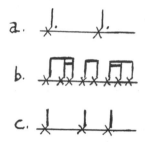

Drums (one high-sounding and one low-sounding) used in this experiment can be especially instructive and interesting.

Did the students discover that—

> . . . different timbres, textures and rhythms often result when a variety of instruments or other sound producing agents performing different rhythms are combined? Depending on the sophistication of the performers and the kinds of instruments used, a kaleidoscope of cross-rhythms, timbres and textures occurs from what first seems to be simple duple or triple patterns.

> . . . rhythmic patterns that are characteristic of much African and Afro-American music should not be thought of as fitting into a strict meter pattern nor should they be performed with a regular metrical accent?

Experience VI.

Experiencing freedom and elasticity of tempo (rubato); creating tension and relaxation; capturing feelings of anticipation and release.

1. Before discussing rubato, listen to "At a Certain Church" from *Scuppernong*, by John Work *(Natalie Hinderas Plays Music of Black Com-*

posers. Desto Records—DC-7102/3) or similar musical selections utilizing clear instances of this performance technique. In "At a Certain Church," the tune "I Am Bound for the Promised Land" will be heard. Have students sing this tune through twice, the first time without the recording and with a steady beat, the second time with the recording, observing the various applications of the rubato technique. What discoveries are made regarding the rhythm? Does the rubato support the musical line? Are the subtle fluctuations in tempo perceived?

Design for Listening

"At a Certain Church"

from *Scuppernong,* by John Work

Events

1   Dissonant chords, clanging church bell effect.

2   Melodic interruption—imitation; clanging continues; fast notes.

3   Chords only; piano echo effect re-enters, slowing ritards to end.

4   Melody, first appearance: middle register, entire verse, smooth (legato) sound, *mf* (note vocal quality of musical line).

5   Melody, second appearance: softer, higher register, variation of first appearance, legato, much slowing and speeding (rubato).

6   Melody, third appearance: summing up—similar to first appearance; brings material from Event No. 1. Much rubato; changing registers; strong closing.

Have the students listen again and conduct various sections. Discuss the results. Is it possible to keep with the performer yet maintain a strict conducting pattern?

Discuss ways in which the pianist is able to capture a quasi-vocal style. Compare this performance to Don Shirley's performance of "Trilogy" (*Gospel According to Don Shirley.* Columbia—CS-9723), another composition based on Negro spirituals (see Experiment No. 2, below). Also listen to "'Easter Monday Swagger: Scherzino" of Thomas H. Kerr, Jr. (on the Hinderas recording). How are these pieces similar? How are they different? To what extent do the performers successfully create feelings of tension and relaxation and elasticity of tempo? Discuss specific places in compositions heard where these characteristics do or do not occur.

2. Listen to "Trilogy" (*Gospel According to Don Shirley.* Columbia—CS-9723), following the suggested "Design for Listening." Have students try to identify the tunes, then sing each one twice, once without and once with rubato. If the tunes are familiar, it might prove interesting to discuss in what situations they had been heard.

Design for Listening
"Trilogy"

Events

Slow tempo

1   Piano: recitative-like; single line on "Glory, glory, hallelujah—when I lays my burden down."

2   Strings join piano; low register, ascending. Piano has hymn tune "Where He Leads Me I Will Follow."

3   Bridge; piano ascends; strings tremolo.

4   Varied and abbreviated repetition of No. 2 in higher register. Much crescendo and decrescendo and rubato.

5   Gregorian chant-like melody in high register of piano over a continuous chord roll in lower register.

6   Tune: "No Mo' Auction Block for Me!" Emphatic presentation; insistent trill on "for." Repetitions; strong cadence.

7   Piano: bass hammers out repetitive single note.

Fast tempo

8   Tune: "If I Had a Hammer." Full ensemble; strong pulse; much contrast between high and low registers. Piano bass patterns play important role. Much crescendo and decrescendo and accents. Typical gospel style.

Listen to Event No. 8 again. How many times was the tune repeated? How is each repetition varied? Discuss other performance and compositional techniques heard. Where else have you heard this pattern? Have students construct their own listening design for this section.

Did the students discover that—

. . . rubato may affect only the melody or the whole musical fabric?

. . . rubato provides an expressive alteration of the steady beat of a composition?

. . . rubato is an effective means of providing tension and relaxation in music? It helps the composer and performer convey subtle and transient feelings.

Experience VII.

Becoming more sensitive to musical characteristics in poetry, noting rhythmic patterns, expressive qualities, timbre, tempo and pulse.

Read each of the following poems.* These poems are among those written by black and Puerto Rican children from Bedford-Stuyvesant, Harlem, Jamaica and the lower west and east sides of Manhattan in New York.

V.B.   Age 14

For what purpose was I born? I don't see.
To speak words that no one will listen to
No matter how loud I shout them?
To throw up dates, and events
just as I recorded them and be pronounced
a genius? To sit through school day after
day and be referred to as a "good child"
To hear things that I shouldn't and then be
instructed to forget?

For what reason am I living? To see
man destroy each other, and we listen
to them preach godlyness and good-will?
To take things as they are and never question?
To live a clean life, only to rot away in your
grave? To have things your soul desires, prohibited?
To be told God is good, but disregard the fact

---

*Reprinted by permission of AVON BOOKS from *The Me Nobody Knows*, edited by Stephen M. Joseph, copyrighted (©) 1969 by Stephen M. Joseph.

that the world—his so called "creation"—
is bad.
But these are thoughts I must
not think if I am to survive.

M.B.   Age 16
When children see you in the summer,
Sun—
          they like you.
They swim, laugh and play,
Sun—
          under your warmth.
But in winter,
sun—
          they lose their affection for you.
You melt their snow
sun—
          they dislike you.
But why
sun—
          must I always have winter?

Clorox (a pen name)   Age 17
What am I?
I have no manhood—what am I?
You made my woman head of the house—what am I?
You have oriented me so that I hate and distrust
My brothers and sisters—What am I?
     You mispronounce my name and say I have no
     self-respect—What am I?
     You give me a dilapidated education system and
     expect me to compete with you—What am I?
     You say I have no dignity and then deprive me
     of my culture—What am I?
     You call me a boy, dirty lowdown slut—
     What am I?
     Now I'm a victim of the welfare system—
     What am I?
     You tell me to wait for change to come, but 400
     years
     Have passed and change ain't come—What am I?

I am all of your sins
I am the skeleton in your closets
I am the unwanted sons and daughters-in-laws, and
rejected babies
I may be your destruction, but above all I am, as
you so crudely put it, your nigger.

Experiment by varying the tempo of reading. Have students identify expressive and rhythmic characteristics such as accents, rubato, articulation, syncopation, tempo and loudness changes, intonation and inflection.

Ask students to study the text and determine specifically how it influences the manner of verbal presentation, through words, complete thoughts, verses or stanzas.

Does a natural flow of the words seem to evolve? Does any one manner seem to have a "rightness" about it? Can you give a feeling of "wrongness" by simply changing word inflections?

What kind of accompaniment do the words (their meaning and sound characteristics) suggest? Experiment with various timbral possibilities by adding instruments to the vocal presentation of the poem.

APPENDICES

APPENDIX A

Black Musicians

This Appendix includes lists of Afro-American musicians whose names and musical contributions should be familiar to music educators. Any disagreement with details of selection or categorization should not be allowed to obscure the basic purpose of this presentation, which is to demonstrate to the reader the scope of successful, creative participation by black musicians in the music profession.

The selection of these names and their placement into categories are determined to a degree according to subjective criteria. Yet varied and specific procedures shaped the selection process.

Many names repeatedly occur in books and articles dealing with Afro-American music that have been annotated in this Source Book and can be consulted by the reader. Record catalogs and discographies were consulted for further evidence of professional accomplishment; the reader is encouraged to sample recordings of many of the musicians listed. A criterion for selection was the consistent mention of names in the authors' conversations with persons having sustained involvement with black music, including individuals associated with black studies programs in several universities.

The musicians who are listed have achieved a noteworthy measure of success in the world of music by virtue of (1) their having attained positions as conductors of or performers in professional organizations such as symphony orchestras or opera companies, or (2) their having contributed significantly to the traditions of gospel, blues, jazz and soul.

The categorization of names was enormously complicated. Musicians merely create music; others tend to categorize their product. Such categorization is defensible when used to orient individuals to unfamiliar and perhaps complex musical terrain. Choices have been made, and readers may revise this material from their own experience.

Concert Music

Names of black composers have been included with dates to assist the reader in placing the composer historically. Recordings of music by many of these composers are available, some of which have been useful to the authors in classes and, therefore, appear in the Afro-American discography (page 82). These lists cannot be considered exhaustive.

Composers

Anderson, Thomas J. (1928-)
Baker, David (1931-)
Bland, James (1854-1911)
Boatner, Edward (1898-)
Bonds, Margaret (1913-)
Bridgetower, George P. (1779-1860)
Brown, J. Harold (1902-)
Brown, Marion
Burleigh, Harry T. (1866-1949)
Chambers, Stephen (1940-)
Charlton, Melville (1883-)
Clark, Edgar R. (1917-)
Coleridge-Taylor, Samuel
  (1875-1912)
Cook, Will Marion (1869-1944)
Cooke, Charles L. (1891-1958)
Cunningham, Arthur (1928-)
DaCosta, Noel (1930-)
Dawson, William (1898-)
De Saint Georges, Chavalier
Dett, R. Nathaniel (1882-1943)
Duncan, John (1913-)
Ellington, Duke (1899-)
Europe, James Reese (1881-1919)
Fax, Mark (1911-)
Fisher, William (1935-)
Freeman, Harry Lawrence
  (1875-1943)
Furman, James (1937-)
Gardner, Newport (1746-1826)
Hailstork, Adolphus C., III (1941-)
Hall, Frederick D. (1898-)
Harris, Robert A. (1938-)
Holland, Justin (1819-1886)
Jeffers, Jack

Johnson, Hall (1888-1970)
Johnson, J. Rosamund (1873-1954)
Johnson, James P. (1891-1955)
Joplin, Scott (1868-1917)
Kay, Ulysses (1917-)
Kerr, Thomas H., Jr. (1915-)
Lewis, John (1920-)
Logan, Wendell Morris (1940-)
McDaniel, William Foster (1940-)
Moore, Carman
Moore, Undine
Nelson, Oliver
Perkinson, Coleridge-Taylor
  (1932-)
Perry, Julia (1927-)
Price, Florence B. (1888-1953)
Price, John (1936-)
Russell, George (1923-)
Ryder, Noah F. (1914-)
Sancho, Ignatius (1729-1780)
Singleton, Alvin
Smith, Hale (1925-)
Still, William Grant (1895-)
Swanson, Howard (1909-)
Thompson, Leon
Tillis, Frederick Charles (1930-)
Walker, Charles (1935-)
Walker, George (1922-)
White, Clarence Cameron
  (1880-1960)
Williams, Henry R. (1813-1889)
Wilson, Olly (1937-)
Work, John Wesley, Jr. (1901-1968)
Work, John Wesley, Sr. (1873-1925)

Instrumentalists

Adams, Armenta—piano
Allen, Sanford—violin
Booth, Alan—piano

Booth, Allan—piano
Charlton, Melville—organ
Cole, Frances—harpsichord

Cooper, Clarence—french horn
Cuney-Hare, Maude—piano
Diton, Carl—piano
Douglas, Joseph— violin
Eaton, Roy—piano
Edwards, Renard—violin
Hagan, Helen—piano
Harreld, Kemper—violin
Haynes, Eugene—piano
Harrison, Hazel—piano
Hinderas, Natalie—piano
Hobson, Ann—harpist
Howard, Fannie—piano
Jeter, Leonard—cello
Jones, Louis Vaughn—violin
Kaufman, Elaine Jones—timpani
Lawrence, William—piano
Laws, Hubert—flute

Lawson, R. Augustus—piano
Lee, Sylvia Alden—piano
Lipscomb, Ron—cello
Madison, Earl—cello
Moore, Kermit—cello
Prattis, Patricia—piano
Ross, Paul—violin
Rowe, Booker—violin
Schuyler, Philippa Duke—piano
Smyles, Harry—oboe
Walker, Francis—piano
Watt, Robert—french horn
Watts, Andre—piano
White, Donald—cello
Wilder, Joseph—trumpet
Williams-Jones, Pearl—piano
Wise, Wilmer—trumpet

Singers

Addison, Adele
Allen, Betty
Anderson, Marian
Arroyo, Martina
Bailey, Therman
Batson, Flora
Bernard, Annabelle
Bledsoe, Jules
Boatner, Edward
Boatwright, McHenry
Brice, Carol
Brooks, Garnett
Brown, Anne
Brown, William
Bumbry, Grace
Cato, Minto
Cole, Celeste
Crawford, Kathleen
Davis, Ellabelle
Davy, Gloria

Dobbs, Mattiwilda
Douglass, Joseph
Duncan, Todd
Dupree, William
Estes, Simon
Evanti, Lillian
Franklin, William
Frierson, Andrew
George, Zelma
Grist, Reri
Hackley, E. Azalia
Hayes, Roland
Holland, Charles
Holloman, Charlotte
Holmes, Eugene
Jackson, Rhea
Jarboro, Caterina
Jones, Sissieretta
Killebrew, Gwendolyn
Lafayette, Leonora

Lee, Ella
Little, Vera
Matthews, Edward
Matthews, Inez
Maynor, Dorothy
McDaniel, Beryl
McFerrin, Robert
Mitchell, Abbie
Monette, LaVergne
Moorefield, Olive
Patterson, Willis
Pierson, Edward
Price, Leontyne
Rahn, Muriel
Ray, William
Richardson, William
Robeson, Paul

Russell, John
Shirley, George
Spearman, Rawn
Spencer, Kenneth
Talbert, Florence Cole
Tyler, Veronica
Tynes, Margaret
Verrett, Shirley
Warfield, William
Watson, Lawrence
Weathers, Felicia
Wentt, Alan
Williams, Camilla
Williams-Jones, Pearl
Winters, Lawrence
Woodward, Sidney
Young, Lauretta

Conductors

Byrd, George
Darden, Charles
DeCoteau, Dennis
DePriest, James
Dixon, Dean
Frazier, James
Freeman, Paul

Harris, Margaret
Jackson, Isaiah
Lee, Everett
Lewis, Henry
Perkinson, Coleridge-Taylor
Porter, Carl Hampton

Performing Organizations

The following performing groups are listed because of their importance in the maintenance of interest both in the black performer and black music. Some of the groups date from the early 1900's, while others are more current.

School Choruses

Alabama State Choir
Fisk Jubilee Singers
Fisk University Choir
Hampton Institute Choir
Hampton Singers
Howard University Choir

Morehouse College Choir
Southern University Choir
Tuskegee Institute Choir
Virginia State College Choir
Wilberforce University Choir

Professional Choirs

De Paur Infantry Chorus
Eva Jessye Choir
Hall Johnson Choir

Leonard De Paur Chorus
Wings Over Jordan Choir

Community Choirs

Harry T. Burleigh Association—
Terre Haute, Indiana
Choral Study Club—Chicago
Coleridge-Taylor Society—
Washington State

Samuel Coleridge-Taylor Choral
Society—Washington, D.C.
Drury Opera Company—New York
Mundy Choristers—Chicago
United Choirs—New Orleans

Orchestras and Bands

Gilbert Anderson Memorial
Symphony Orchestra
Baltimore City Colored Orchestra
Camden Negro Symphony
Desdunes Band
Harlem Philharmonic

Lyre Club Symphony Orchestra
Oakland Youth Symphony
Philadelphia Anderson Orchestra
Symphony of the New World
Victorian Concert Orchestra

Vaudeville and Musicals

The following list includes musicians involved in vaudeville and musicals from the turn of the century through the 1920's.

Performers

Baker, Josephine
Jarboro, Caterina
Mills, Florence
Rainey, Gertrude "Ma"

Robeson, Paul
Robinson, Bill "Bojangles"
Waters, Ethel

Directors

Cook, Will Marion

Composers

Blake, Eubie
Bland, James
Bradford, Perry
Brooks, Shelton
Brymn, Tim
Cole, Robert
Creamer, Henry S.
Dabney, Ford
Handy, W. C.
Hill, J. Leubrie
Johnson, Hall
Johnson, J. Rosamund

Johnson, James P.
Jordan, Joe
Layton, J. Turner
Pinkard, Maceo
Roberts, Charles "Luckey"
Rogers, Alex C.
Sissle, Noble
Vaughn, James
Vodery, Will
Waller, Fats
Williams, Clarence
Williams, Spencer

Motion Picture or Television (1930's to the present)

Composers

Bishop, Walter, Jr.
Carter, Benny
Davis, Miles
DeJesus, Luchi
Ellington, Duke
Gillespie, John Birks "Dizzy"
Golson, Benny
Hancock, Herbie
Hayes, Isaac
Hopkins, Kenyon
Jackson, Calvin
Johnson, J. J.

Jones, Booker T.
Jones, Quincy
Lewis, John
McIntosh, Thomas
Mingus, Charles
Monk, Thelonius
Nelson, Oliver
Parks, Gordon
Redd, Freddie
Rollins, Sonny
Thompson, Lucky

Gospel

All of the following singers, pianists, songwriters, gospel choirs and ensembles are well known or are important historically. The reader may know of many other gospel artists or groups which could be added to this list.

Abyssinian Gospel Choir of Newark
Alex Bradford Singers
Angelic Gospel Singers
Anderson, Robert
Art Reynolds Choir
Barrett Singers
Birmingham Jubilee Singers

Bolden, Alfred
Bowles, Lillian
Brewster, Reverend W. Herbert
Brown, Shirley
Caravans
Ceasar, Shirley
Clara Ward Singers

Clark, Mattie Moss and the
 Southwest Michigan State Choir
Cleveland, James
Cooke, Sam
Davis, Reverend "Blind" Gary
Davis Sisters
Delta Rhythm Boys
Dixie Hummingbirds
Dorothy Norwood Singers
Dorsey, Thomas A. "Georgia Tom"
Dunklin, Hulah Jean
Edwin Hawkins Singers
Five Blind Boys
Five Blind Boys of Alabama
Five Blind Boys of Mississippi
Franklin, Aretha, Carolyn and Erma
Franklin, Reverend C. L.
Frye, Theodore
Garden State Choir of Newark
Georgia Peach
Beverly Glenn Chorale
Golden Gate Quartet
Gospelaires
Gospel Clefs
Gospel Harmonettes
Griffin, Bessie
Harmonizing Four
Harold Smith Majestics
The Humming Birds of Greenville,
 South Carolina
Institutional Church of God In
 Christ
Jackson, Mahalia
James Cleveland Singers

Jessy Dixon and the Chicago
 Community Choir
Johnson, Blind Willie
Kings of Harmony
Martin, Roberta
Martin, Sallie
Matthews, Lucy "Little Lucy"
Mighty Clouds of Joy
Morris, Kenneth
Norfolk Jubilee Singers
Raymond Rasberry Singers
Richmond Harmonizing Four
Roberta Martin Singers
Roberts, Reverend Lawrence
Sensational Nightingales
Stars of Faith
Staple Singers
Soul Stirrers
Southernaires
Tharpe, Sister Rosetta
Thrasher Wonders
Utterbach Ensemble of New York
Wallace, Rosie
Walter Arties Chorale
Watkins, Reverend Charles
Ward, Clara
Webb, Willie
White, J. T.
Wilson Harmonizers of North
 Carolina
Williams, Marion
Williams, Wallace and the Howard
 University Gospel Choir

Blues

Composers

(in addition to most of the performers listed under the various blues
categories)

Bradford, Perry
Handy, W. C.

Williams, Clarence

Performers

Early Blues

Jefferson, Blind Lemon
Johnson, Blind Willie
Morton, Ferdinand "Jelly Roll"

Rainey, Gertrude "Ma"
Wheatstraw, Peetie

Classic Blues (1920's)

Austin, Lovie (Cora Calhoun)
Cox, Ida
Hill, Bertha "Chippie"
Hegamin, Lucille
Hunter, Alberta
Martin, Sara(h)
Rainey, Gertrude "Ma"
  ("Mother of the Blues")
Smith, Bessie ("Empress of the
  Blues")

Smith, Clara ("Queen of the
  Moaners")
Smith, Mamie (pop singer; first
  recorded blues)
Smith, Trixie
Spivey, Victoria
Wallace, Sippie
Waters, Ethel

Country Blues (1920's to the present)

Alexander, Texas
Anderson, Pink
Barbecue Bob (Robert Hicks)
Broonzy, Big Bill (William Lee
  Conley)
Cadillac, Bobby
Cannon, Gus
Dupree, Champion Jack
Fuller, Blind Boy (Fuller Allen)
Fuller, Jesse
Glinn, Lillian
Hooker, John Lee
Hopkins, Sam "Lightnin' "
House, Son
Howell, Peg Leg
Hurt, Mississippi John
Jefferson, Blind Lemon
Johnson, Blind Willie

Johnson, Robert
Ledbetter, Huddie "Leadbelly"
Lewis, Furry
Lipscomb, Mance
Mack, Ida May
McDowell, Fred
McGhee, Walter Brown "Brownie"
McTell, Blind Willie
  (or "Blind Sammie")
Slade, Wilk "Son"
Tate, Baby
Terry, Sonny (Saunders Teddell)
Tucker, Bessie
Walton, Wade
Waters, Muddy (early in career)
White, Bukka
Williams, Robert "Pete"

Urban Blues (1920's to the present)

Ace, Johnny
Big Maybelle (Mabel Smith)
Blake, Blind (Arthur)
Bland, Bobby (early in career)
Broonzy, Big Bill (William Lee
   Conley)
Brown, Charles
Brown, Roy
Campbell, Little Milton
Carr, LeRoy and Scrapper Blackwell
Fulson, Lowell
Gordon, Roscoe
Guy, Buddy
Hooker, John Lee
Hopkins, Sam "Lightnin'"
Howlin' Wolf (Chester Burnett)
Hunter, "Ivory Joe"
Jackson, Benjamin Clarence
   "Bullmoose"
Johnson, Lonnie
Jordan, Louis
King, Albert

King, Freddy
King, Riley "B. B."
Lenoir, J. B.
Memphis Minnie
Memphis Slim
Merriweather, Big Maceo
Milburn, Amos
Moore, Gatemouth
Parker, Junior
Reed, Jimmy
Rush, Otis
Sykes, Roosevelt
Tampa Red (Hudson Whittaker)
Taylor, Little Johnny
Thornton, Willie Mae "Big Mama"
Turner, Joe
Walker, Aaron "T-Bone"
Washington, Dinah
Waters, Muddy (McKinley
   Morganfield)
Williamson, John Lee "Sonny Boy"
Witherspoon, Jimmy

Shouting Blues (1930's and 1940's)

Brown, Walter
Harris, Wynonie
Hibbler, Al
Jordan, Louis
Page, Hot Lips
Rushing, Jimmy "Little" or
   "Mr. Five-by-Five"

Stidham, Arbee
Turner, Joe
Vinson, Eddie "Cleanhead"
Williams, Joe
Witherspoon, Jimmy

Popularized Blues (1940's and 1950's)

Belafonte, Harry
Bibb, Leon
Eaglin, Snooks
Johnson, Buddy

Odetta
Washington, Dinah
White, Josh

Rhythm and Blues (1940's to the present)

Ace, Johnny
Baker, LaVern
Ballard, Hank and the Midnighters
Benton, Brook
Berry, Charles Edward "Chuck"
Bland, Bobby
Brown, Charles
Brown, James
Brown, Maxine
Brown, Roy
The Cadets
Chandler, Gene
The Chantels
Charles, Ray
The Charts
The Clovers
The Coasters
Cooke, Sam
Crayton, Pee Wee
Curtis, King
Davis, Eddie "Lockjaw"
The Dell-Vikings
The Diamonds
Diddley, Bo
The Dixie Cups
Dixon, Floyd
Domino, Antoine "Fats"
The Drifters
The El Dorados
The Five Royals
The Five Satins
Franklin, Aretha
Fulson, Lowell
Gant, Cecil
Gordon, Roscoe
Harris, Peppermint
Harris, Wynonie
The Heartbeats
Hibbler, Al
Hogg, Smokey

Hooker, John Lee
Hope, Lynn
Hopkins, Sam "Lightnin' "
Jackson, Chuck
Jackson, Benjamin Clarence
    "Bullmoose"
Jackson, Willis "Gatortail"
The Jaguars
James, Etta
Johnson, Ella
Jordan, Louis
King, Ben E.
King, Freddy
King, Albert
King, Riley "B. B."
Little, Richard
Little Willie John
Mayfield, Percy
McDaniels, Gene
McNeeley, Big Jay
McPhatter, Clyde
The Medallions
Milburn, Amos
Moore, Gatemouth
The Orioles
The Penguins
Parker, Junior
The Platters
Price, Lloyd
The Ravens
The Rays
Redding, Otis
Scott, Freddie
The Shields
Shep and the Limelites
Simon, Joe
Smith, Huey "Piano"
The Spaniels
Sykes, Roosevelt
The Teen Queens

Tex, Joe
The Turbans
The Velvetones
Thornton, Willie Mae "Big Mama"
Turner, Joe
Walker, Aaron "T-Bone"
Washington, Dinah "The Queen"

Ward, Billy and the Dominoes
Waters, Muddy
  (McKinley Morganfield)
Williams, Maurice and the Zodiacs
Williamson, John Lee "Sonny Boy"
Wilson, Jackie
Witherspoon, Jimmy

(For additional listing of Rhythm and Blues artists,
refer to Soul category, page 142.)

Cry Singers

Brown, James
Hinton, Joe
Little, Richard

Mitchell, McKinley "The Soul"
Tex, Joe

"White" Blues

Beatles
Butterfield, Paul
Guthrie, Woody
Joplin, Janis

Monroe, Bill
Righteous Brothers
Rodgers, Jimmie
Rolling Stones

Blues in Jazz Idiom

Allison, Mose (white)
Armstrong, Louis
Morton, Jelly Roll
Rawls, Lou
Rushing, Jimmy

Vaughan, Sarah
Washington, Dinah
Williams, Joe
Witherspoon, Jimmie

Jazz

The following names are included to assist the music educator to become familiar with some of the major contributors to the jazz tradition. Categories of jazz styles are presented in approximate chronological order, recognizing that styles may have overlapped or occurred simultaneously. In addition, it must be kept in mind that musicians move readily from one area to another, resisting categorization; for this reason, some musicians are listed in more than one category. Others appear only in the idiom in which their contribution was widely recognized. Still others appear in the category of "Other Performers" because of their extreme diversity of styles.

Since this Source Book deals with black music, it could be expected that only black artists would appear. However, several white musicians have been included (and indicated as white) in this section of the Appendix. This was done for two reasons: (1) jazz is the first idiom in which there was historical communication between black and white musicians, and (2) certain jazz styles were adopted mainly by white musicians.

Early Jazz Musicians
(active professionally prior to the 1950's)

New Orleans Musicians (1890's to 1920's)

Armstrong, Louis—trumpet
Baquet, George—clarinet
Baquet, Theogene—trumpet/cornet
Barrett, Emma—piano
Bechet, Sidney—
    soprano saxophone/clarinet
Bolden, Charles "Buddy" or
    "King"—cornet
Celestin, Oscar "Papa"—trumpet
Chandler, Dee Dee—drums
Dodds, Johnny—
    clarinet/alto saxophone
Dodds, Warren "Baby"—drums
Dusen, Frank—trombone
Dutrey, Honore—trombone
Eureka Brass Band
Excelsior Brass Band
Foster, George "Pops"—bass
Galloway, Charles "Happy"—guitar
Hardin, Lil (Armstrong)—piano
Humphrey, Jim—cornet
Jackson, Dewey—trumpet/cornet
    (riverboat bands)
Johnson, Buddy—trombone
Johnson, William Geary "Bunk"—
    cornet/leader
Jones, Richard Myknee—
    composer/arranger/piano
Keppard, Freddie—
    cornet/trumpet/leader

Kimball, Henry, Sr.—bass
Ladnier, Tommy—trumpet
Lewis, Frank—clarinet
Lewis, George—clarinet
Lindsay, John—bass/trombone
Marable, Fate—leader
    (riverboat bands)
Mitchell, George—cornet
Morton, Ferdinand "Jelly Roll"—
    piano/composer
Nelson, Louis "Big Eye"—clarinet
Noone, Jimmie—clarinet
Oliver, Joseph "King"—cornet/
    trumpet/composer/arranger
Ory, Edward "Kid"—trombone
Perez, Manuel—cornet
Picou, Alphonse—clarinet
Pierce, Billie and "Dee Dee"—
    piano and trumpet
St. Cyr, Johnny—banjo/guitar
Scott, Arthur "Bud"—guitar/banjo
Simeon, Omer Victor—clarinet
Tio, Lorenzo, Jr.—clarinet
Tio, Lorenzo, Sr.—clarinet
Tio, Luis—clarinet
Williams, Black Benny—drums
Young Tuxedo Brass Band
Zeno, Henry—drums

Ragtime (1890's to World War I)

Blake, James Hubert "Eubie"—
    piano/composer
Blake, Shout
Botsford, George (white)—composer
Chauvin, Louis
Europe, James Reese—composer
Green, Big Jimmy
Hayden, Scott—composer
Henry, Plunk
Hunter, Charles (white)—composer
Johnson, Charles L. (white)—
    composer
Joplin, Scott—composer

Jordan, Joe
Lamb, Joseph (white)—composer
Marshall, Arthur
McLean, Richard "Abba Labba"
Nelson, "Slew Foot"
Patterson, Sam
Pickett, Jesse
Scott, James—composer
Sewell, Willie "Egg Head"
Turpin, Thomas Million
Weinrich, Percy (white)—composer
Wilbur, Big-Head

New York (Harlem) "Stride" Piano (1910 to 1930)

Johnson, James P.
Roberts, Charles "Luckey"

Smith, Willie-the-Lion
Waller, Thomas "Fats"

Northern Black Orchestras and Bands (before and during World War I)

Adams, Alton Augustus—
    Navy Band
Brymn, Tim—Army Band
Cook, Will Marion—orchestra
Duff, George—Army Band
Europe, James Reese—
    Army Band and orchestras
Howard, Wesley—Army Band

Rhodes, Dorsey—Army Band
Sissle, Noble—composer
    (Europe's Army Band)
Thomas, Jack—Army Band
Thompson, Egbert—Army Band
Tyers, William H.—orchestra
Vodery, Will—
    Army Band and orchestras

Blues Piano— "Boogie-Woogie" (World War I to late 1930's)

Ammons, Albert
Davenport, Charles "Cow Cow"
Johnson, Pete
Lewis, Meade Lux
Lofton, Cripple Clarence

Montgomery, Eurreal "Little
    Brother"
Smith, Clarence "Pine Top"
Thomas, Hersal

Big Bands (from the early 1920's)

Allen, Henry "Red"—trumpet
Anderson, Ivy—singer

Anderson, William "Cat"—trumpet
Armstrong, Louis—trumpet/

singer/composer/arranger/leader
Bailey, William "Buster"—clarinet
Baker, Harold "Shorty"—trumpet
Basie, William "Count"—piano/
composer/arranger/leader
(Kansas City)
Beiderbecke, Leon Bismarck "Bix"
(white)—cornet
Blanton, Jimmy—bass
Calloway, Cabell "Cab"—
leader/singer/arranger
Carney, Harry—baritone sax
Carver, Wayman—
flute/alto saxophone
Cook, Will Marion—
composer/arranger
Creath, Charlie—trumpet
(riverboat band)
DeParis, Wilbur—trombone
Ellington, Duke—leader/piano/
composer/arranger (Washington,
D.C.)
Ellington, Mercer—
composer/arranger/trumpet
Fitzgerald, Ella—singer
Greer, William Alexander
"Sonny"—drums
Guy, Fred—drums/banjo/guitar
Hardwicke, Otto "Toby"—
alto/baritone saxophone
Harrison, Jimmy—trombone
Hawkins, Erskine—leader/trumpet
Hawkins, Coleman—
tenor saxophone
Henderson, Fletcher—piano/
composer/arranger/leader
(New York)
Higginbotham, Jay C.—trombone
Hines, Earl "Fatha"—piano
(Chicago)

Hite, Les—leader (Los Angeles)
Hodges, Johnny—alto saxophone
Hopkins, Claude—leader
Johnson, Pete—piano
Kirk, Andy—piano/leader
(Kansas City)
Lunceford, Jimmie—leader
(Memphis)
McShann, Jay—leader (Kansas City)
Miley, James "Bubber"—trumpet
Millinder, Lucky—leader
Morrison, George—leader (Denver)
Moten, Bennie—leader
(Kansas City)
Nance, Ray—trumpet/violin
Nanton, Joseph "Tricky Sam"—
trombone
Oliver, Joseph "King"—
cornet/leader
Page, Walter—leader (Kansas City)
Parrish, Avery—piano
Redman, Don—saxophone/arranger
Reinhardt, Django (Belgian)—guitar
Russell, Luis—leader (Chicago)
Smith, Bessie—singer
Stone, Jesse—leader (Kansas City)
Strayhorn, Billy—piano/composer
Tate, Erskine—leader (Chicago)
Teagarden, Jack (Weldon John)
(white)—trombone/leader
Vodery, Will—composer
Webb, William "Chick"—
drums/leader
Webster, Ben—tenor saxophone
Williams, Charles Melvin
"Cootie"—trumpet
Williams, Joe—singer
Young, Lester "Pres"—
alto/tenor saxophone

Swing (mid-1930's to mid-1940's)

Barnet, Charlie (white)—
    leader/alto, tenor, soprano sax.
Basie, William "Count"—
    leader/piano/composer/arranger
Carter, Benny—alto saxophone
Catlett, Big Sid—drums
Christian, Charlie—guitar
Clayton, Wilbur "Buck"—trumpet
Crosby, Bob (white)—leader
Dorsey, Jimmy (white)—
    leader/clarinet/alto saxophone
Dorsey, Tommy (white)—
    leader/trombone
Eldridge, Roy—trumpet
Ellington, Duke—
    leader/piano/composer/arranger
Goodman, Benny (white)—
    leader/clarinet
Gray, Wardell—tenor saxophone
Greer, William Alexander
    "Sonny"—drums
Hampton, Lionel—
    leader/vibraphone

Hawkins, Coleman—
    tenor/alto saxophone
Henderson, Fletcher—
    piano/composer/arranger
Henderson, Horace—
    arranger/piano/leader
Herman, Woody (white)—
    clarinet/leader
Hill, Teddy—leader/saxophone
Holiday, Billie "Lady Day"—singer
James, Harry (white)—
    trumpet/leader
Miller, Glenn (white)—
    leader/trombone
Norvo, Red (white)—vibraphone
Oliver, Melvin James "Sy"—trumpet
Rich, Buddy (white)—drums
Shaw, Artie (white)—leader/clarinet
Stacy, Jess (white)—piano
Williams, Charles Melvin
    "Cootie"—trumpet
Wilson, Gerald—leader/trumpet
Wilson, Teddy—piano

Dixieland (mid-1940's)

Condon, Eddie (white)—
    leader/guitar/banjo
Crosby, Bob (white)—leader
Johnson, Bunk—trumpet

Lewis, George—clarinet
Nichols, Red (white)—trumpet
Ory, Edward "Kid"—trombone
Watters, Lu—leader/trumpet

Other Performers

Addison, Bernard—guitar/banjo
Berry, Leon "Chu"—
    tenor saxophone
Bigard, Leon "Barney"—clarinet
Braud, Wellman—bass
Bunn, Teddy—guitar/banjo
Casey, Albert Aloysius—

    guitar/banjo
Cole, William "Cozy"—drums
Coleman, Bill—trumpet
Dunn, Johnny—trumpet
Evans, Herschel—tenor saxophone
Hall, Adelaide—singer
Hall, Edmond—clarinet

Hamilton, Jimmy—clarinet
Hill, Alex—composer/arranger
Howard, Darnell—clarinet/violin
Humes, Helen—singer
Jones, Jo—drums
Jones, Jonah—trumpet
Kirby, John—bass/leader
McPartland, Jimmy (white)—
    trumpet (Chicago)
Morgan, Al—bass
Mundy, Jimmy—composer/arranger
Norman, Fred—composer/arranger
Sampson, Edgar—
    composer/arranger/saxophone
Singleton, Arthur James "Zutty"—
    drums

Smith, Cladys "Jabbo"—trumpet
Smith, Hezekiah Leroy Gordon
    "Stuff"—violin
Smith, Joe—trumpet
South, Eddie—violin
Stewart, Leroy "Slam"—bass
Tatum, Art—piano
Ware, Leonard—guitar/banjo
Wells, Dickie—trombone
Williams, Mary Lou—
    piano/composer/arranger
Wilson, Robert Edward "Juice"—
    violin/clarinet/alto saxophone
Wynn, Albert—trombone

Recent Jazz Musicians
(active professionally since approximately 1945)

Bop (1940's)

Ammons, Gene—tenor saxophone
Blakey, Art—drums
Brazil, Joe—tenor/alto saxophone
Burns, Ralph (white)—
    piano/composer
Christian, Charlie—guitar
Clarke, Kenny "Klook"—drums
Coltrane, John—tenor saxophone
Dameron, Tadd—piano/composer
Davis, Miles—trumpet
Dorham, Kenny—trumpet
Eckstine, Billy—singer/leader
Gaillard, "Slim"—guitar
Getz, Stan (white)—saxophone
Gillespie, John Birks "Dizzy"—
    trumpet
Gordon, Dexter—tenor saxophone
Green, Benny—
    trombone/saxophone
Green, Urbie (white)—trombone
Harris, Benny—trumpet

Harris, Bill (white)—trombone
Hawkins, Coleman—
    tenor saxophone
Hefti, Neal (white)—
    arranger/trumpet/piano
Hinton, Milt—bass
Jackson, Milton "Bags"—vibraphone
Johnson, Budd—
    tenor saxophone/arranger
Johnson, J. J.—trombone/composer
Mitchell, Red (white)—bass
Monk, Thelonious—piano
Moody, James—saxophone/flute
Navarro, Theodore "Fats"—trumpet
Nichols, Herbie—piano
Parker, Charlie "Bird"—
    alto/tenor saxophone
Parker, Leo—baritone saxophone
Potter, Tommy—bass
Powell, Earl "Bud"—piano
Roach, Max—drums

138

Sims, Zoot (white)—
  tenor/alto saxophone/clarinet
Stitt, Sonny—
  tenor/alto/baritone saxophone
Thompson, Eli "Lucky"—
  tenor saxophone

Valentine, Jerry—
  arranger/trombone
Vaughan, Sarah—singer/piano
Wilson, Shadow—drums
Young, Lester "Pres"—
  tenor saxophone

Progressive Jazz (late 1940's)

Graettinger, Bob (white)—composer
Kenton, Stan (white)—piano/leader

Raeburn, Boyd (white)—leader

Cool Jazz (late 1940's to mid-1950's)

Baker, Chet (white)—trumpet/singer
Brubeck, Dave (white)—piano
Clarke, Kenny—drums
Davis, Miles—trumpet
Desmond, Paul (white)—
  alto saxophone
Evans, Gil (white)—arranger
Getz, Stan—tenor saxophone
Jackson, Milt—vibraphone

Konitz, Lee (white)—alto saxophone
Lewis, John—composer/pianist
  (Modern Jazz Quartet)
Mulligan, Gerry (white)—
  baritone saxophone/arranger
Roach, Max—drums
Tristano, Lennie (white)—piano
Winding, Kai (white)—trombone

Hard Bop (late 1950's)

Adderley, Julian Edwin
  "Cannonball"—alto saxophone
Adderley, Nat—trumpet
Blakey, Art—drums
Coltrane, John—
  soprano/alto/tenor saxophone
Davis, Miles—trumpet
Golson, Benny—tenor saxophone
Jones, Elvin—drums

McLean, Jackie—alto saxophone
Mingus, Charles—
  composer/bass/piano
Monk, Thelonious—piano
Rollins, Sonny—tenor saxophone
Silver, Horace—piano
Smith, Jimmy—organ
Terry, Clark—trumpet

Third Stream (late 1960's)

Ellis, Don (white)—leader/trumpet
Giuffre, Jimmy (white)—saxophone
Lewis, John—composer/piano
  (Modern Jazz Quartet)

Schuller, Gunther (white)—
  composer

Avant-garde (1960's to the present)

Ayler, Albert—saxophone
Ayler, Don—trumpet
Bell, Charles—piano/composer
Brown, Marion—alto saxophone
Byrd, Donald—trumpet
Cherry, Don—trumpet
Coleman, Ornette—alto saxophone
Coltrane, John—tenor saxophone
Davis, Miles—trumpet
Dolphy, Eric—woodwinds
Haden, Charlie (white)—bass

Higgins, Billy—drums
Hubbard, Freddie—trumpet
Lloyd, Charles—saxophone
Mingus, Charles—composer/bass
Rollins, Sonny—tenor saxophone
Saunders, Pharaoh—
    tenor saxophone
Shepp, Archie—tenor saxophone
Sun Ra and the Solar Arkestra
Taylor, Cecil—piano
Tyner, McCoy—piano

Other Performers

Ammons, Gene—tenor saxophone
Betts, Keter—bass/drums
Brown, Clifford—trumpet
Brown, Ray—bass
Brown, Oscar, Jr.—singer
Burrell, Kenny—guitar
Byrd, Charlie (white)—guitar
Carter, Ron—bass
Chambers, Paul—bass
Charles, Dennis—drums
Clark, Sonny—piano
Cobb, Arnett—tenor saxophone
Cobb, Jimmy—drums
Cole, Nat "King"—piano/singer
Coltrane, Alice—piano
Cooper, Buster—trombone
Crawford, Hank—saxophone
Criss, Sonny—alto saxophone
Curson, Ted—trumpet
Davis, Richard—bass
Davis, Sammy, Jr.—singer
DeJohnette, Jack—drums
Booker Ervin Quintet
Evans, Bill (white)—piano
Farmer, Art—trumpet
Flack, Roberta—singer/piano
Garner, Erroll—piano

Garrison, Jimmy—bass
Gray, Wardell—tenor saxophone
Green, Grant—guitar
Griffith, Earl—vibraphone
Grimes, Tiny—guitar
Hamilton, Chico—drums
Hancock, Herbie—piano
Handy, John—woodwinds
Harley, Rufus—bagpipes
Harris, Eddie—tenor saxophone
Hart, Billy—drums
Hawes, Hampton—piano
Hawkins, Erskine—trumpet/leader
Haynes, Roy—drums
Heath, Percy—bass
Holiday, Billie—singer
Horn, Paul (white)—flute
Horne, Lena—singer
Hutcherson, Bobby—vibraphone
Jamal, Ahmad—piano
Johnson, Joe—drums
Jones, Joe "Philly"—drums
Jones, Thad—trumpet/flugelhorn
Kelly, Wynton—piano
Kloss, Eric (white)—
    tenor/alto saxophone
Lateef, Yusef—woodwinds

Laws, Hubert—flute
Lyons, Jimmy—alto saxophone
Mann, Herbie (white)—flute
McCann, Les—piano
McDuff, Jack—organ/bass/piano
McIntyre, Ken—woodwinds
McRae, Carmen—singer
Mitchell, "Blue" (Richard Allen)—
   trumpet
Mobley, "Hank" (Henry)—
   tenor saxophone
Montgomery, Buddy—piano/vibes
Montgomery, Monk—electric bass
Montgomery, Wes—guitar
Morgan, Lee—trumpet
Newborn, Phineas—piano
Newman, Dave "Fathead"—
   tenor saxophone

Owen, Jimmy—trumpet
Pepper, Art—alto/tenor saxophone
Peterson, Oscar—piano
Priester, Julian—trombone
Redd, Freddie—piano
Shorter, Wayne—
   tenor saxophone
Staton, Dakota—singer
Taylor, Billy, Jr.—piano
Terry, Clark—trumpet
Turrentine, Stanley—saxophone
Williams, Anthony—drums
Williams, Buster—bass
Williams, Mary Lou—
   piano/composer/arranger
Williams, Richard—trumpet
Wilson, Nancy—singer
Zawinul, Josef (white)—piano

Soul

Soul is the music that occurs when gospel music, blues and jazz are blended in any combination. Lists of soul artists are extremely difficult to compile. The reader is free to disagree with the classifications. The application of categories itself forces vague divisions and placements. Music educators who were consulted on this matter, however, indicated that some categorization would be valuable in the preliminary exploration of soul music.

We have tried to overcome some of the worst problems by using a variety of divisions in which artists will sometimes appear more than once. Although names of performers and groups are used, it will be obvious that listening to recordings of these artists will not insure that the specified category, or genre, is represented. As one persists in listening, however, it will become obvious which genre particular selections exhibit. Students should be encouraged to provide assistance in guiding listening and furnishing other examples.

Again, these lists are merely representative. Hopefully, they will provide some idea of the scope of Afro-American music in which so much activity can be seen. The first three lists (including both individuals and groups) are presented in approximate historical order; the following eleven are arranged according to predominating influences in sound or genre. Two lists include names of several white persons and groups who have adopted or have been influenced by soul music.

Gospel

This representative list contains individuals and groups who began, in performance and certain recordings, to make the transition between gospel and soul.

Charles, Ray
Cooke, Sam
The Drinkard Singers (with Dionne Warwick)
Franklin, Aretha
The Gospelaires (with Dionne Warwick)
Jackson, Mahalia
Little Milton
McCann, Les

Pickett, Wilson
Rawls, Lou
Reese, Della
Simone, Nina
The Soul Stirrers (with Sam Cooke and Johnnie Taylor)
The Staple Singers
Taylor, Johnnie
Warwick, Dionne
Washington, Dinah

Rhythm and blues (1950's and early 1960's)

This list includes representative artists or groups who made a transition between blues and soul with some jazz and gospel influence.

Baker, LaVerne
Ballard, Hank
Berry, Chuck
Bland, Bobby
Brown, Ruth
Charles, Ray
Checker, Chubby
The Clovers
The Coasters
Conley, Arthur
Cooke, Sam
The Corvettes (with Arthur Conley)
Diddley, Bo

Domino, Fats
The Dominoes
The Drifters
The Five Royals
The Flamingoes
Little Anthony and the Imperials
Pickett, Wilson
The Platters
Price, Lloyd
The Radiants
The Swallows
Wilson, Jackie

Soul (1960's)

The Bar-Kays
Brown, James
Brown, Oscar, Jr.
Charles, Ray
Cropper, Steve (white)
Floyd, Eddie

The Four Tops
Franklin, Aretha
Gaye, Marvin
Gladys Knight and the Pips
Hayes, Isaac
The Impressions

The Jackson Five
Jones, Booker T.
Lewis, Ramsey
Little Richard
Mayfield, Curtis
The M.G.'s (with Booker T. Jones
    and Steve Cropper)
Pickett, Wilson
Porter, Dave
Rawls, Lou

Redding, Otis
Simone, Nina
Sly and the Family Stone
Smokey Robinson and the Miracles
Taylor, Johnnie
Thomas, Carla
Turner, Ike and Tina
Warwick, Dionne
Wonder, Stevie

Influences

These lists are arranged around predominating influences within the subdivision of soul music.

Motown sound

Four Tops
Gaye, Marvin
Jackson Five
The Miracles
Martha Reeves and the Vandellas
Smokey Robinson and the Miracles

Diana Ross and the Supremes
Temptations (David Ruffin)
Terrell, Tammi
Wells, Mary
Wonder, Stevie

Memphis sound

Bar-Kays
Floyd, Eddie
Hayes, Isaac
Jones, Booker T. and the M.G.'s
    (Steve Cropper and Donald
    "Duck" Dunn)

Porter, David
Redding, Otis
Sam and Dave (Sam Moore and
    Dave Prater)
Staple Singers
Taylor, Johnnie
Thomas, Carla

Blues — gospel — soul

Bland, Bobby
Brown, James
Brown, Oscar, Jr.
Charles, Ray
Franklin, Aretha

Pickett, Wilson
Rawls, Lou
Simone, Nina
Taylor, Johnnie

Blues — soul

Thomas, Rufus
Washington, Dinah

Wells, Junior

Adderley, Julian "Cannonball"
Adderley, Nat
Flack, Roberta
Harris, Eddie
Holmes, Richard "Groove"
Jones, Quincy
Kearney, David "Guitar Shorty"

Lewis, Ramsey
McCann, Les
Montgomery, Wes
Silver, Horace
Smith, Jimmy
Washington, Dinah
Zawinul, Joe (white)

Rock — soul

Hendrix, Jimi

Country — western — soul

Pride, Charlie

Latin American performers

The following musicians are representative of those who have contributed to the jazz and soul traditions as a result of their background and training which reflect black musical influences within Latin America.

Bobo, Willie
Feliciano, José
Machito (Frank Grillo)
Pozo, Chano (Luciano Gonzales)

Prado, Perez
Puente, Tito
Santamaria, Mongo
Santana, Carlos

White performers

The following are names of white performers who have adopted soul or who are said to be "soul singers." Because they have been strongly influenced by many of the soul traditions, they have developed a unique style; thus, their names are placed in this separate category. This list does not include many other rock groups which have been affected by soul music but are not considered to be soul singers.

The Beatles
Bishop, Elvin
Bloomfield, Mike
Butterfield, Paul
Clapton, Eric
Everly Brothers
Gentry, Bobbie
Hammond, John, Jr.
Jones, Tom

Joplin, Janis (Big Brother and the
  Holding Company)
Mayall, John
Nyro, Laura
Parker, Gene
Presley, Elvis
The Rascals
Righteous Brothers
Rolling Stones

APPENDIX B

General Reference Books and Materials

Bibliographic Survey: The Negro in Print. Washington, D.C.: The Negro Bibliographic and Research Center, Inc., 1965-

Black Bibliography: a Selected List of Books on Africa, Africans, and Afro-Americans. Long Beach, Calif.: California State College, 1969.

Black List. New York: Panther House, Ltd., 1970.
A concise reference guide to publications and broadcasting media of black America, Africa and the Caribbean. Addresses are provided for newspapers, periodicals, broadcasting stations, colleges and universities, publishers, book stores, book clubs, literary agents and embassies relating to blacks in these geographical locations.

Ellis, E. M. V. *The American Negro: A Selected Checklist of Books.* Washington, D.C.: Howard University Library (Washington Negro Collection), 1968.

Feather, Leonard. *The New Edition of the Encyclopedia of Jazz.* New York: Horizon Press, 1960.

Feather, Leonard. *The Encyclopedia of Jazz in the Sixties.* New York: Horizon Press, 1967.

Fisher, Mary F. (comp.). *The Negro in America: A Bibliography.* 2nd edition revised. Cambridge, Mass.: Harvard University Press, 1970.

Folk Music: A Selection of Folk Songs, Ballads, Dances, Instrumental Pieces and Folk Tales of the United States and Latin America—Catalog of Phonograph Records. Washington, D.C.: Library of Congress, Music Division, Recording Library, 1959.

From Slavery to Protest: A Bibliography of Afro-American Resources for the Pennsylvania Schools. Harrisburg: State Department of Education, Division of School Libraries and Social Studies, 1968.

Gaskin, L. P. J. *A Select Bibliography of Music in Africa.* Compiled at the International African Institute under the direction of K. P. Wachsmann. London: International African Institute, 1965.

Gillis, Frank, and Alan P. Merriam. *Ethnomusicology and Folk Music: An International Bibliography of Dissertations and Theses.* Middletown, Conn.: Wesleyan University Press, 1966.

Hamer, Philip M. (ed.). *A Guide to Archives and Manuscripts in the United States.* New Haven, 1961.

Jahn, Janheinz. *Bibliography of Neo-African Literature from Africa, America and the Caribbean.* New York, 1965.

Kennedy, Peter (ed.). *Films on Traditional Music and Dance, First International Catalog.* Compiled by the International Folk Music Council, London. Paris: UNESCO, 1970.

Kruzas, Anthony T. (ed.). *Directory of Special Libraries and Information Centers.* Detroit, Michigan, 1963.

Leadbitter, Mike and Neil Slaven. *Blues Records: 1943-1966.* London: Hanover Books, 1968.

A List of American Folksong Currently Available on Records. Washington, D.C.: The Library of Congress, Music Division, Archive of American Folk Song, 1953.

McCarthy, Albert, *et al. Jazz on Record: A Critical Guide to the First 50 Years.* London: Hanover Books, 1968.

Merriam, Alan P. *African Music on LP: An Annotated Discography.* Evanston, Illinois: Northwestern University Press, 1970.

Merriam, Alan P. and R. Benford. *A Bibliography of Jazz.* Philadelphia: The American Folklore Society, 1954.

Music Educators Journal. "Bibliography," Vol. 56 (January 1970), p. 113.

The Negro American in Paperback: A Selected List of Paperback Books Compiled and Annotated for Secondary-School Students. Washington, D.C.: National Education Association, 1967.

The Negro Spiritual (bibliography). Washington, D.C.: Library of Congress, Music Division, Archive of American Folk Song, 1970.

The Philadelphia Library Company. *Negro History: 1553-1903.* Philadelphia: The Winchell Company, 1969.
    An annotated bibliography of an exhibition of books, prints and manuscripts from the shelves of the Library Company of Philadelphia and the Historical Society of Pennsylvania. The source includes actual prints (reproductions) and reproductions of rare manuscripts. It is more than a bibliography in that it is highly readable with ample photos to give interest. The Library Company of Philadelphia and the Historical Society are located at 1300 and 14th Locust Streets, Philadelphia.

Porter, Dorothy. (comp.). *The Negro in the United States: A Selected Bibliography*. Washington, D.C.: Library of Congress, 1970.

Reisner, Robert T. *The Literature of Jazz: a Selective Bibliography*. New York: New York Public Library, 1959.

Roxon, Lillian. *Rock Encyclopedia*. New York: Workman Publishing Company, 1969.

Salk, Erwin A. (comp.). *A Layman's Guide to Negro History*. Enlarged edition. New York: McGraw-Hill, 1967.

Shetler, Donald J. *Film Guide for Music Educators*. Washington, D.C.: Music Educators National Conference, 1968.

Szabo, Andrew (comp.). *Afro-American Bibliography*. San Diego, California: San Diego State College Library, 1970.

Thieme, Darius L. (comp.). *African Music: A Briefly Annotated Bibliography*. Washington, D.C.: Library of Congress, Music Division, 1964.

Turner, Darwin T. *Afro-American Writers*. New York: Appleton-Century-Crofts, Educational Division, Meredith Corporation, 1970.
    A source intended for graduate and advanced undergraduate students of literature wanting a guide to literature and the literary scholarship of Afro-Americans. References to related topics such as history, art, music, journalism and folklore. Critical studies of uses of African and Afro-Americans as characters in American literature are included.

Welsch, Edwin K. *The Negro in the United States, A Research Guide*. Bloomington, Indiana: Indiana University Press, 1965.

Winchell, Constance M. *Guide to Reference Books*. 8th edition. Chicago, 1967.

Work, Monroe N. *A Bibliography of the Negro in Africa and America*. New York: H. W. Wilson, Co., 1928. Reprinted: Tuskegee Institute, 1965.